David Brooks is the author of five previous collections of poetry and several novels and works of short fiction. His *The Book of Sei* (1985) was heralded as the most impressive debut in Australian short fiction since Peter Carey's. His novel *The Fern Tattoo* (UQP, 2007) was shortlisted for the Miles Franklin Literary Award. *The Sydney Morning Herald* called his collection of poetry, *The Balcony* (UQP, 2008), 'an electric performance'. Until 2013 he taught Australian Literature at The University of Sydney. In recent years he has devoted his writing increasingly to animal advocacy. He lives with rescued sheep in the Blue Mountains of New South Wales. In 2014 he was awarded a 2015/16 Australia Council Fellowship for services to Australian and international literature. *The Other Side of Daylight* was the Poetry winner of the 2025 Prime Minister's Literary Awards.

Also by David Brooks

Novels

The House of Balthus
The Fern Tattoo
The Umbrella Club
The Conversation

Short Fiction

The Book of Sei and Other Stories
Sheep and the Diva
Black Sea
Napoleon's Roads

Poetry

The Cold Front
Walking to Point Clear
Urban Elegies
The Balcony
Open House

Non-fiction

The Necessary Jungle: Literature and excess
De/scription: A Balthus notebook
The Sons of Clovis: Ern Malley, Adoré Floupette, and a secret history of Australian poetry
The Grass Library
Derrida's Breakfast
Animal Dreams: Selected Essays
Turin: Approaching Animals

Translation

The Golden Boat: Selected poems of Srečko Kosovel
(with Bert Pribac)

David Brooks

The other side of daylight

New and Selected Poems

First published 2024 by University of Queensland Press
PO Box 6042, St Lucia, Queensland 4067 Australia
Reprinted 2025

University of Queensland Press (UQP) acknowledges the Traditional Owners and their custodianship of the lands on which UQP operates. We pay our respects to their Ancestors and their descendants, who continue cultural and spiritual connections to Country. We recognise their valuable contributions to Australian and global society.

uqp.com.au
reception@uqp.com.au

Cover design by Design by Committee
Cover photograph by David Brooks
Author photograph by Teja Brooks Pribac
Typeset in 11.5/14 pt Adobe Garamond Pro by Post Pre-press Group, Brisbane
Printed in Australia by McPherson's Printing Group

University of Queensland Press is assisted by the Australian Government through Creative Australia, its principal arts investment and advisory body.

A catalogue record for this book is available from the National Library of Australia.

ISBN 978 0 7022 6828 1 (pbk)
ISBN 978 0 7022 6938 7 (epdf)

University of Queensland Press uses papers that are natural, renewable and recyclable products made from wood grown in well-managed forests and other controlled sources. The logging and manufacturing processes conform to the environmental regulations of the country of origin.

Contents

III

FROM *Open House* 2015

FROM *The Balcony* 2008

FROM *Urban Elegies* 2007

FROM *Walking to Point Clear* 2005

FROM *The Cold Front* 1983

NEW POEMS

The Peanut Vendor[1] 2016–2023

to Andrew Burke (1944–2023), poet,
for this collection's title and forty years of friendship

I

Wild Duck Sutra

Eight wild wood ducks
greet me at the gate,
follow me down to the feed-room, wait
while I get them a handful of seed
before taking hay to the sheep
who descend upon it as if it were the last
lucerne in the country

I stand and watch
then leave them to it, walk off
to fill the water trough
the sky clearing
in more ways than meet the eye
the world outside these fences
so precariously at bay

it hardly bears thinking: all
things are full of meaning, so
they say, you just
have to wait for it;
what they don't say
is how much you have to clear away
before the simplest things become evident

as this, for example,
dripping from the tank-lip,
creeping like sunlight
over the grass,
slipping from beaks of wood ducks, how
we might share refuge, rescue
each other

The Night Coming

I was thinking it was cold, the heater
struggling against the draught,
and that there was nothing I could say, how
empty my mind was,
but then looked up and saw you
working in the paddock in the thin rain in your black
jacket against the almost-
evening of the trees
with the white dog at heel,
and the four sheep grazing about you,
and the sounds, through the mist, of cockatoos
settling in high branches,
the wood-shed in its winter sleep,
five wild ducks
moving in single file through the grass.

TABLELANDS

after Ian Dodd's Mirror Image *(1975)*[2]

High on the tableland,
in a shallow valley, by the entrance
to an abandoned diamond mine
amongst discarded machinery and

empty oil drums, a broken
aerial, long past redemption, hums
in the stiffening breeze
above the pillaged cabin

of a great earthmover
beside a darkened shed,
rusted water tank
and tiny lean-to over

the latrine on a clearing where,
in an ancient caravan,
the old caretaker and a pair
of visitors drink bourbon

and, with stones for money, play
lazy poker late into the night, the dove-
white bowl of the moon low above them
big as half the sky.

Invitation

It's another of those everything-is-full-
of-everything-else-every-thingpart-of-which-
is-full-of-everything-else-so-that-no-
thing-is-itself-therefore-everything-
is-full-of-nothing-nothing-is-
everything kind of days, the field
full of mist and silent but for the occasional
creak of crow or crow from the
rooster on the farm below, the sheep
deep in their sheepness and the ducklings
eyeing me attently as though
there's a secret between us I've
totally forgotten or perhaps never
understood in the first place, the old
dog staring at me from the open door as if
in invitation, but where to? where?

Stolen Lemons

i.m. Martin Harrison

Someone has come into our yard
and stolen all the lemons from our tree.
It had been giving us such pleasure
to watch them glow in the evening

like lanterns amongst the dark leaves, be
able to take, whenever we needed, two or three.
It is hard to know what to feel; anger
doesn't seem quite appropriate. There's clearly

another who loves lemons as much as we; I too
might have been tempted to steal a few
had I seen such a sight as these had been,
atop a sheltered rise, on a deserted street.

Had it been the sheep I might have understood,
since sheep also love lemons, but as it is
I've no idea. A whole crop, a hundred
yellow globes or more, daffodil-bright,

with a scent that, when the breeze was right,
you could pick up almost a block away.
In truth I don't know if I'd have mentioned them
had it not been for hearing, just yesterday,

that a man, a poet I'd known, had died.
We were not close, but, as some people seem to be,

were quietly at ease in each other's company
whenever we found ourselves by chance together,

and spoke, once or twice, of human things – heart-
problems, aches in our bones, the changing weather –
as if there'd been mutual care.
When I look at my lemon tree now, so

bare in the half-light
without their glowing there,
it's hard not to think that an almost-friend
hasn't also been stolen somehow.

Bower Bird

Someone has been eating the peaches
with Mukimono finesse – not
the white cockatoos, who most likely
would have taken one bite and left the rest to rot, or,
balancing deftly on one leg, turned the plucked fruit
carefully in the other claw
until they'd finished the lot, but a bird
with a taste for miniature, diadem. At first
I thought green finches, or blue wren,
but no: today, as I was watering potato-plants,
my mind a hundred miles away, I became aware
of a grey-green movement in the shade
and saw her there, my old
friend from this time last year, lured
back by the scent, I guess,
to tell me what I'd already seen – how
ripe the flesh was, with such a golden sheen –
pecking at a fallen peach with such
thoughtful precision you'd think her
unaware I was near, though in truth
she'd stop, every few seconds, and glance,
as if as concerned to hold my stare
as I was to keep her there – then, her
meticulous serration done, she cast
one long last look and, low, as if
heavy with nectar or
encounter, flew.

LINDEN

after Edward Thomas, 'Adlestrop'

Linden? The station? Yes, I remember
The sign, because early one Saturday,
Unexpectedly, the Bathurst train lay
Briefly over there. It was late November.

The doors opened. Someone coughed.
No one boarded or stepped off
Onto the long, quiet platform. What I saw
Was 'Linden', nothing more,

Except golden coreopsis, long rows
Of dry sansevieria, a few clouds high
In the pale sky. And for those
Few moments, near-by,

I heard a currawong call,
And around her, it seemed, in bands
Ever wider and wider, all
The birds of the Central Tablelands.

Farewell to the Long Sad Party

The long sad party is ending.
No one is listening to the poets, or spending
any time with the philosopher.
No one is trying to understand
the lyrics of the gypsy band.

The long sad party is ending.
No one is visiting the terrace gallery
to see the famous painter's
pictures of apocalypse.
No one is reading the novelist.

The long sad party
is ending as it has always done.
The dancers on the balcony
hold one another and move gently
then turn away.

The voices of the singers
drift along the corridors,
the golden wine is poured, and poured again,
someone murmurs
something about a morning train.

Outside, on the darkened lawn,
under the last whisper of the midnight moon,
a woman turns to her lover.
She opens her mouth to her
and they fall and fall.

Booth Street

I wanted to say
that when you left
the warmth went out of the sun.
For the first two days
I had such trouble
with the unexpected cold.
But this afternoon, at almost sunset,
the light on Booth Street was so bright
not one of us driving towards it
could see where we were going, nor knew
whether to stop, or how.

Woman Dancing

See the woman dancing
in the kitchen late at night, a glass
of wine in her hand and the tears gone, the windows
full of darkness reflecting her.

See the woman
dancing with the music on
softly so as not to wake
the sheep, the dog, her
husband in the bed two rooms away.

See
the woman dancing, watch
her softly sway, the great
moon and the gentle night, the spiders
in the corners, moths and
forest insects
flocking to the pane.

Snapper Island

He'd made motions to leave at ten
but stayed talking until almost one
about the spiders in the mountains
and the lyrebirds he'd seen
the week before, a pair
so busy gossiping as they'd wandered
down the ravine they hadn't seen
him watching – the late
planes passing high overhead, the occasional
moan from a freighter
negotiating Snapper Island.

The taxi when he called it
arrived almost immediately
but we talked on after he'd gone
an hour or so more
of the last part of which I remember
almost nothing, so tired I was
after so much wine; only
waking at four,
hearing the sounds of your breathing,
the absolute stillness.

Parable of the Tins

Reading in my two-by-three metre brick-
paved, weed-infested, inner-
urban backyard I see a letter curiously
detach itself from a footnote

to crawl towards the bottom right-
hand corner of the page and realise
it's an insect of a species
I have never seen before, and, too late

to prevent my finger from
flicking it away, though just in time
for that sort of miniature cataclysmic state
we fondly call revelation, rise

and walk towards the pile of paint tins
stacked in the passageway beside the bins
waiting to be collected by the guys
from the Sydney City Council's

Toxic Waste Disposal Centre,
and, down on my knees, turn over
a rock that might have been lying there
a year or perhaps a decade now, and look, I

mean really look, as much as my
incipient presbyopia allows, and, sure enough,
there are two, three – seven! – more
creatures I have never seen before, not of that

but of a different kind, and I start to wonder
if, under this rock, these, then what
under the next rock and the rock after that
or under the paint tins and plant pots – under

and in them, if I were to trawl
my fingers carefully through the soil? Then think
of drains, of downpipes, spider webs
I brush off almost weekly from the

clothes pegs on the line, and ... well, I
could go on but guess the point is made
or certainly was to me, a universe
I'd have said I'd always known about

but would as usual have been lying without
knowing it, but knowing, now, something,
and I looked around and it was
rush hour in the passageway, ants

heading everywhere for home, birds
conducting intricate conversations
on the guttering overhead, plants
breathing languages I do not

and could never know. Were I a
saint or something I would
pack up my bag
and go.

Easter 2016

—W.B. Yeats, 'Easter 1916'

It's Easter, and the butcher shops
are full of carcasses of lambs. My wife
is reluctant to leave the house for fear
someone will steal
our own lamb from the field,
though she herself wants to liberate
rabbits from the cages people this year
are putting out on their front lawns
in some bizarre new Easter ritual – to give them
refuge, keep them
safe from The Devouring.

It's Easter, and a man
has stabbed to death his lover
in full view at a downtown shopping mall; a suicide
bomber has just killed
seventy mourners at a
funeral in Lahore and another lying
Australian politician
has just resigned his leadership: Easter,
and a Royal Commission
has yet again delayed
reporting on the suffering of thousands of children
who came or were blindly
sent to Him

and were sexually
assaulted by clergy.

It's
Easter, 2016: let's
take our chance alone; let's
not mark our door-posts;
let's not roll away the stone

let's
not molest our children, let's
not devour
the gentle creatures we live amongst

let's
stop, for Christ's sake, let's
stop.

Foxes

After dinner and the washing-up, we go outside
to sit on the deck, the evening chilly but dry, the sky
overcast, no visible stars. Someone
is holding a party nearby, playing
something vaguely familiar.
In the breaks between songs
we hear marsh frogs, crickets, the padding
of a ring-tailed possum on the roof, the siren
of an ambulance somewhere, traffic
on the highway, a woman
singing in the dark
in a house across the road.

At 4 am, the night
now almost silent,
I get up, needing a pee. The clouds
have cleared, the light
from a full moon
is filling the house.
I stand there
at the bathroom window
watching for a minute or so
wondering how the party went, how
the revellers got home, where
the drivers on the highway
might have been going, how
the patient in the ambulance, the woman
in the house across the road might be, think
of the sheep

in their coop below the fence, the possum
in the cedar tree,
go back to bed
and to sleep again,
dream of foxes.

II

Coronary

Coasting down the hillside
to the highway and the hospital in Izola,
the sweat pouring off me, the ambulance
having declined to come, we see
two deer
in an olive grove beside the road,
their wide eyes,
flashing
in the headlights,
slipping so
quickly into night.

The Forest Next Door

Dead then, 7.30 am, poems
doubtless already in your wake
running round in the forest with a knife
after a heavy night's drinking
determined to kill ■ whom you say
has stolen your writing pay
stalking in circles through the spotted gums
or coming up from the ■ wharf
with fresh-caught bream
I could taste the water still lapping in
then drinking, drinking, watching
Rage till almost dawn
with you and ■ on the double bed
the pair of you a few months later
bashing the heck out of one another
stark naked in my living room at 3 am
talking and talking
poetry with its dark insidious mysteries
old love old pain old theft again
the death season, as ■ said yesterday
outside the chemist on Katoomba Street

what the ■ have you done now?

nothing to do
but get on with it, the endless
Poem still caught in the teeth
light pouring down outside

currawongs
shrieking in the forest next door

Taralga Road

Early spring, gold
wattle lining the lanes, dams
brimming, fields
emerald-green
clotted with long-eared lambs, road
pot-holed from the winter rains,
a motorcyclist
come a cropper
being loaded into an ambulance
just north of the old asylum.

'Wombat,'
she announces,
and stops, gets out.
I watch her in the rear-view
turn the body over, jog back
for gloves, a cloth, the first-aid kit. 'She's
dead,' she says, 'but there's
a tiny paw
reaching from the pouch. I've
got to check.'

Across the road, two
young black steers, ears
blue-tagged for slaughter,
amble to the fence, then others
and still more, a dozen, twenty, eyes
wide in concern; if they weren't
animals you'd almost think they knew her, this

baby dead also, pale
and fur-less,
barely filling the palm of her hand.

Three kilometres further there's another. 'Their pouches
are so wet,' she murmurs, then talks in awe
of the size of their teeth, their claws. By Oberon
there have been two more
and almost a dozen roos. Some
we stop at, others you can just tell
it's far too late, or there's
a truck on your tail, or the road's so narrow
there's no space to pull over
let alone run.

Near Jenolan, dusk coming on,
we stop at a young swamp wallaby, head
crushed by a kerbside wheel, the road
a single lane, then, our
examination done, step
back to allow a four-wheel drive to pass, watch
as it grinds her – eyes, ears, brain –
deeper into the bitumen. Her joey
who'd been still breathing
dies in our hands.

Passports

Animals don't have passports, although
in Australia, to move a 'farm' animal
from one 'animal processing plant' to another,
you must have that animal fitted
with a plastic identification tag, attached
through a hole punched in his or her ear.
I refer, of course, to *non-human* animals: *human*
animals in Australia may move wherever they like, unless
they are illegal immigrants who've been
caught and imprisoned in what *non*-Australians might call
concentration camps, but which Australian government officials
refer to as Offshore Processing Centres.

I recently heard of a cow who,
wandering into a neighbour's field,
unwittingly crossed the border between
one Central European country and the next. She
was arrested. Only an international outcry, led
by Sir Paul McCartney, saved her from execution.

The common barn swallow, an astonishing bird,
flies up to eighteen thousand kilometres each year
on its migration to and from southern Africa,
a great many of them pausing, as they cross the Mediterranean,
to rest on the islands of Malta and Lampedusa.

In October, 2013, a boatload of human refugees, attempting
to do much the same, caught fire and capsized five
hundred metres offshore, drowning almost all on board.

An ice-cream seller from Lampedusa, sleeping
on a yacht nearby, said he was awakened by the sound
of what at first he thought to be birds.

Many people drown at sea as they try to reach
what they hope will be the coasts of refuge. Thankfully
some of them reach safe harbour.
I could say more – about the bravery
of rescuers and rescued alike, let's say – but perhaps
I've said too much already. Non-
human animals may be rescued
from industrial farms, and stricken travellers, although
prison-bound, may be saved from drowning
in the Mediterranean or Andaman or Timor Sea,
but the oceans of our immense stupidity
threaten and diminish us all.

It's safer to talk about swallows …

Plague Night

Late March, cold
and overcast, cockatoos
loud at dusk then
silence, heavy
rain at three, a rat
gnawing at the wire
over the new exhaust-fan duct
wearing her teeth to no purpose,
keeping me awake
until at least three-twenty when, heard
by no one, everyone, someone
burns loudly down the road outside,
trying to kill some
helpless creature, possibly himself.

On a Photograph of Sheep Killed by Bushfire

Trapped by barbed wire
they have had
no way to go
between the fence and the wall of fire

each of the twenty-seven
now swelling in the Thursday sun, face
blackened, body savagely shorn
caught on the track between

camera and a gutted ute,
the driver fled,
now safely in a nearby town
lamenting his loss of livelihood

in the foreground
the open eyes
of the bell sheep
staring through clambering flies

Late Love Poem

I can't say why
I don't seem to grieve anymore

not my father whose face I carry
and whose voice speaks so often through my own

not my mother who's come back for me
in lover after lover

not even my friends, older and younger,
lost to time, or death, neglect – some

inability to love in me it has been said
or deep repression

but what would others know?
If I lost you, I would not mourn, there'd

be no time:
I would just go.

Overcast

Overcast, a weak
front passing through, and whether it's
because he raised himself so long alone
in a muddy swamp behind a brickyard
or some other, darker, black-sheep thing
I can only ever guess about,
Jason, as is his wont,
is standing calmly in the rain, eyes
partly closed and
breathing evenly, gone
somewhere deep inside himself, ruminating
in both senses of the word, his head, with
every in-breath and
exhalation
moving slowly from side to side
as if to say, over and over,
No, no, no, no, no …

On Reading of Another Slaughter

It's a grey day, full of rain,
the sheep have been coming out
to graze in the intervals, and at the end
of the long road outside the kangaroos
will have been sheltering in the thin forest
by the old sewage works.

On the *ABC News* I've just read
about hundreds of magpie geese
yesterday shot dead and
dumped
in a 'popular hunting reserve' near Darwin.

It'd be hot up there.
The carcases will already
be rotting in the sun.
The open season's
just begun, apparently,
but there are rules: each hunter
can only 'bag' five geese
and they must take the breast and thighs.

I should be used to these things by now.

The geese
in the accompanying pictures
are not wearing bags.
They all have
pink feathers on their breasts and

bellies.
Their wings
spread and
feet trailing behind them, it's as if
they are flying upside down, carrying
the whole world on their shoulders.

There's a great
trench below me.

Sometimes I think I am falling.

Wild Weather

i.m. Rob Jones

A huge wind yesterday
blew out a window in the writing room, and down
in the city a string of wild dust-storms
has been turning everything red. We've
had rain every second day or so
for almost a month now but more often than not
it stops at the edge of the mountains;
in Bathurst, the lucerne guy tells me,
they're still deep in drought.

The sheep for the most part weather it
at the foot of the verandah stairs, though in a lull
might wander off to graze the sheltered spot
around the back of the house.

It's all
part of a vast symphony, I'd tell them if
I could, by Shostakovich most likely: mighty
batterings, great crescendos, skeins and
fugal progressions, small
wisps of melody or sudden
silences,
some of them haunting.

Pig

Who would write of a pig
and what would a pig know of Spirit?

Who would think that the soul of a pig,
as it leaves the pig's body,
would create the slightest disturbance in air?

What would a pig know of agony?

What would a pig know of death?

The screaming of a pig
shredding the air above a village
is no more than the sound
a heavy table makes
as it is dragged across stone.

The motionlessness
of a sow in a birthing stall
is no more than a pig at rest

the groaning
only the closing
of a metal door
far off inside her.

One Too Many Mornings

I don't remember what it was, I guess
just one too many mornings
reading an item in the early news
telling of yet another skirmish or

outright assault in the endless war,
an unknown killer scattering cubes
of poisoned meat in a local park, a new
target set for the culling of roos

another ship leaving Fremantle
with seventy thousand sheep aboard
destined for eventual slaughter,
but in exasperation, writing to a friend

I'd mentioned the Auschwitz of the Animals
only to receive a leaden reprimand.
'How can you compare,' she asked, 'the suffering
of animals with the suffering of humans?'

I've considered this carefully and, ironically,
have come to think she may be right: there's
the Auschwitz of humans, one
of the lowest episodes in the long

and foetid history of our race,
and there are these other, ordinary things
with no particular name or place,
these 'natural', daily things we do, the wrenching

of children from their mothers, the stealing
of milk to feed the children of others,
the maceration of infants or severing
of body-parts alive, the trucking

of countless creatures to their deaths – over
no stock-race, no paddock gate, no sty
that indefensible lie,
Arbeit Macht Frei.

Afternoon of the Fauns

Mid-afternoon, white
cockatoos
ripping fruit from the peach tree,
council workers up on Mort Street
mending pot holes after all the rain
and a poem has just passed through, gone
almost as soon as I noticed it, over
on Albion Street by now most probably
inspecting someone's pile
for the large-item garbage collection – an old
exercise bike with as-new seat and pedals,
or a box of dented pots and a baking tray,
a bookshelf emptied of its cargo of thought –
or maybe still around here somewhere after all
distracted by the scarlet breasts
of lorikeets
deep as the dress of a woman I once saw
in a painting in Derek's studio
standing on a balcony, overlooking one of those
fields of corn
he told me always symbolised
absolute confusion,
the memory of the two orphaned fauns
who woke me in his spare room
the morning after we arrived, their liquid eyes
so huge I could have walked right into them.

Leaping Towards Boston

(Six hundred kangaroos run the Boston Marathon, 2019)[3]

Tearing through ti-tree, fanning out through brigalow,
boxing and weaving, the young kangaroos
are training for the challenge of their lives,
running through the evening light,
leaping towards Boston in the southern night,
crashing and plashing through gidgee and saltbush,
red gum and spear grass, banksia, wandoo,
leaping with their cousins, their mothers,
their aunts and their tiny brothers,

leaping towards the lights and guns,
racing through the nets of stars
bounding towards the skinners' knives,
bounding though the hide is torn
screaming from their backs and thighs,
pounding along highways in the cold pre-dawn
to the tanners in Narangbar, Yallourn,
crates bound for China, Thailand, Vietnam,
running from their battered bodies, their shattered mobs

towards the frames, the lasts, the stitchers' bobs,
leaping towards Boston, riding on the loaded decks
of container ships, over massive swells of ocean,
through swirling birds and plastic-ridden wracks
towards the docks and training camps,
towards the Main Street starting ramps,

every fifth competitor a roo
running for Reebok, Nike, Adidas,
past Ash and Ray Streets, Wilson, keeping pace

with the fastest, pushing the forward packs,
leaping for the smashed skulls and shattered backs
of siblings, pounding the hills of Newton, racing down
to Beacon and Hereford, crashing through
the final banner, dazzling the camera crew.
What? You can't see them, can't *see* them, there
on the podium, the winner's stand? Amongst
the ghostly carcasses, the blood-stained feet?
Can't see them? Can't *see* them? No?

Winter Gardening

I must plant the garlic and onions
and so today, a late-autumn Saturday, watched
keenly by magpies anticipating a feast,
am on my knees at the garden's edge,
turning soil, scattering slaters,
disturbing tiny emeralds of moss, pushing in
and lifting with a sharp-edged trowel
lump after lump of moist black earth,
knocking the tangled, filamentous roots of weeds
against the old stone border, scattering clotted
dirt into short-cropped grass, pulling up
long, invading chains of couch and mint, removing
cutworms, wrenching out the dead
stumps of tomato vines, eggplants, zucchini,
exposing craters of unimagined busyness, covering
the writhing of creatures revealed so clumsily to light,
ignoring ants and spiders, millipedes and inchworms
struggling over sudden, uneven ground,
digging deep for the pale corms of onion grass,
wondering at the teeming darkness, feeling
World in my brute fingers, Eye
on my shoulders, pausing
in sudden, sad appal, praying
mutely to the god of worms
for forgiveness, please, forgiveness.

The Grip

A glossy black cockatoo
hangs upside down
in the scrub below the fence,
tearing apart the tight new
cones of a she-oak, then takes off
towards Wentworth, caught
by the last of the sunset,
bursting into flame;
all evening
an unsettling wind
bringing wood-smoke, wild fire.

Around midnight
something heavy
lands on the tin roof, takes
off again. Rats
gnaw at the skirtings,
the lights
of our neighbours
go out.

Whatever it is
that is holding us here,
love, emptiness,
flexes, tightens its grip.

Spider Night

Morning warm and dry for once
and spider webs everywhere,
hanging from the branches of trees
slung across the feed-room door
covering the paddock gate.
Makes you wonder if there might be
such a thing as a spider night, moon
low and bright to the west
plenty of small winged creatures about
slant of the light
almost perfect
breeze just right.

Romanée-Conti

It's October 15th 2018 and a bottle of Romanée-Conti 1945
just sold for 785,000 dollars.
Rotting bodies are being dug by hand from earthquake rubble
in Sulawesi because the local government didn't have
the money for the earthmovers that could have shifted
the soil and debris while people were still alive
and a bottle of Romanée-Conti 1945 burgundy just sold
for 785,000 dollars.
Elephants in India, in their dozens, are being shot and
skinned by poachers
to provide ingredients for a new range of Chinese perfumes;
kangaroos are being dragged from earthen dams
in their hundreds because of the continuing drought;
remote Indigenous communities in Western Australia
are being shut down
because the government finds it too expensive to provide
essential services; poisoned falcons and wedge-tailed eagles
are dropping out of the Mallee sky, and 85,000 children
have died so far from famine in Yemen.
People are suffering; animals are suffering; the trees
and the fields and the deserts are suffering; theft
and exploitation are everywhere
and there's so much that we might do to help
and a bottle of Romanée-Conti 1945 burgundy just sold
for 785,000 dollars; that's
104,666 dollars per standard glass. The saddest
and most appalling thing is that although by now
it will probably taste like an old priest's piss,
the price sounds about right.

Trying to Make Something Happen

4 am, a cool
breeze through the open shutters

a large
dog
on the far side of the village
barking incessantly
trying to make something happen

I'm here alone!

Answer me!
Answer me!

III

The Peanut Vendor

They come back, nowadays,
at noon and again at four
as they wander down to graze; you might almost say
it has been set in stone: they
with their loud knockings to call me from my desk – their
sidelong glances, their rubbing themselves
on the sheep-worn edges of the door –
along with the magpies who dart in
for fragments about their hooves
and the cabin rat, who cleans up by starlight
and who once, as I sat
motionless
in the pleasure of the winter sun,
came to my foot, and touched it, with her delicate
paws, almost as if
she felt the same wonder.

Gang-Gang

Warren Osgood's new sidekick
has come to check the septic, all the way
from Cobbitty and it's only nine
down there ten minutes and off again
to the next customer
in Leura, Wentworth, Lawson.
Cold, windy, threatening rain

a gang-gang
clambering about in the foliage
of a big peppermint next door
bright orange head
diving over and over
into the depth of it
coming up blazing.

An Invasion of Clouds

My study has just been invaded by clouds
each smelling vaguely of lanolin and urine,
soft-eyed, wet-nosed, curious-tongued,
come to inspect my books and papers,
like tax collectors for the invisible
or auditors from the ineffable earth
trying to determine how I waste my time.
Their leader, the unicorn, wants to taste
the volume of poems in my lap, while another
makes for the unfiled bills, the third
stares at the ancient aquatint
of my great-grandmother in her wedding dress,
and the fourth, the black one, turning his back,
slowly and sensually rubs his behind
on the literary theory section of the bookshelf.
Following the others out,
he pauses at the doorframe for a final scratch
then pees with pleasure on the just-washed floor.

Peace

While I'd written a mist had descended,
I looked up, and the far trees, the houses, the valley had gone
and there were just us, and the sheep in the field, the house;
one of the rams looked up, and seemed
to murmur something, and a crow crossed,
and I watched, and thought, and went back to my writing.

Requiem

On the 26th of October last year, 5 am,
I heard, for half an hour, an unfamiliar bird-call,
and tried to record the shape of it
in my notebook in the bedroom dark.
At 10.55 that morning, meteorologists now say,
a bolt of lightning from a dying storm
struck a bone-dry stringybark
deep in that part of the national park
they call the Devil's Wilderness,
igniting a fire that burned unreachable through the day.
At 7.10 pm our beloved dog Charlie, riddled with cancer,
  struggled
to his feet beside our outdoor table
and tried to get inside. We picked him up
and took him to his place beside the bed.
Five minutes later, as if some large invisible creature
had placed their knee in the middle of his spine
and, hand beneath his jaw, pulled him
backward like a longbow, he reared
then bent slowly, gently forward
and took no further breath. By the middle
of that night the fire
had burned five hundred hectares. Un-
stoppable through November, December, January, it became
the largest bushfire this country's ever seen. No
human died but no one knows
how many animals it killed; day after day whole
flocks of birds incinerated in mid-flight; day after day
whole families of wallabies, wombats, possums

outrun by flame. Burnt leaves and embers
fell from the air. There were fires across town, fires
on our own road. Our bags were packed. We lived
in constant readiness, but what is that? I said
goodbye to books, to photographs, to papers, gave
in my mind
so much of my life away
it seemed I'd found a new lightness
like a second, fire-hardened skin, astonished yet again
at how little our vast lives boil down to; each of us
confronting our essential isolation, walking through.

When at last it came, the heavy rain
that extinguished the exhausted blaze
almost on our doorstep turned our lower acre
into an image of the Zambezi River. That
was February; four weeks later
the virus had come; my being
one of those at risk, we spent the next
eight months completely shut away. I've not
gone to the fire-ground
but – gang-gangs, whistlers – watched refugees come.

It's
spring now, fire-
season again. Last week
my young granddaughter, wearing
a red fire-jacket and hard plastic hat,
led me out to the garden to see
the blaze on the bottlebrush, the purple
torches of lavender, the deep crimson blooms
of the camellia, knocked to the ground by the wattlebirds

and smouldering in the thick new grass,
saying *shshsh, shshsh* as she pulled the trigger
of her magic extinguisher, putting out each flame.

It's
spring, October, cicadas
are tunnelling up from the roots of the cherry tree, ducklings
fossick in the vegetable beds, the sheep
need shearing, the lemons
are bright over Charlie's grave.
This morning
I heard that bird again.
I still don't know its name.

The Other Side of Daylight

Well here we are
and the world
is large again, places
a little more themselves again

the life around us
strange once more
the simplest things
difficult like before

wolves
walk out from the forests
emus wander the empty streets
grass appears in unexpected places

desires
are forbidden again
longing
bristles on our skin

the stillness
holds us close
silence
almost fills the mind

skies
blaze again with a billion stars
scents of long-forgotten places
arrive on the night wind

How Yesterday

... at the end
of an overcast morning, just
before the sun reappeared, two
of the four sheep, Jason
and Henry, came
into my writing room
for peanuts and to sip
at the water bowl,
and how Henry, after Jason left,
came over and stood beside me
at the desk, and stayed ten
minutes while I stroked his cheek
as if to acknowledge, each of us,
that we knew something
we couldn't ever say
except by the silence there
breathing the same air.

Lament for Fieldmice

I believe in no deity
and the religion I was born into
is dangerous and hollow as a drum,
but I won't accept that these great trees I stand among
are not the volutes and capitals
of a vast, inconsecrate cathedral, or that Henry
the used-to-be ram is not high priest,
the ducks and cockatoos and currawong
apostles and prophets of a different sky,
the rats and fieldmice the local
council has just poisoned – who'd bring
me whispers as they passed –
mystics and hapless seraphim
now twisting in agony in the summer grass.

Trees

Every now and again you find yourself
standing on the edge of something, not quite
knowing what it is, the
slope, for example, above the swamp, a hundred
metres or so below the house. When we came here
there were giants there, either
side of the fence-line, enough to screen
almost entirely the suburb opposite – thick, shaggy stringybarks, rough-
coated peppermints, monumental mountain ash – and
over the years, at the top of the paddock, from the window
of my writing room, I've seen several of them go,
brought down by wild winds or their own weight, the ground
no longer strong enough to hold them.
                                        I don't know
what it was, exactly, whether the angry sound
of chainsaws from the common land, or the death
of yet another friend, but late last week
I went down to stand
among the few that are left of them, my first
visit in too long a time, the slope
steeper than I remembered, my legs and balance
not what they were, but I did it, and stood there,
in a grove she's made from the sectioned
trunk of a fallen messmate. Dusk
was coming on, the last of the late-autumn sun
reddening the cloud over the eastern spur. A crowd
of sulphur-crested cockatoos flew
raucously northward and came raucously back, crows
dipped and glided high above us, kookaburras

kick-started their angelus, the air
was sharp and pure, full of swamp and reed and eucalyptus
and I saw that, in the three years since I'd been there
the bush had thickened, what was then
scrub was now almost forest, what were saplings were now
tall slender trees, with generous rustling canopies, bark
of living silver, and I turned and breathed and turned
and breathed again, the three
sheep watching, then, reluctantly, lest dark
catch up with me, in a chill, stiffening breeze, with greater
difficulty than I'd expected, made my way
back to the house, and that evening, by a warm
heater, thinking of this, drank
wine, though I'm told I shouldn't, rich,
deep and intense, full
of night and memory and black berries – *terror*, as a mis-
printed label once said – telling myself
they are just trees,
only trees,
but …

Visitor

You come to visit me in the mountains
on a day of bells and wood-smoke, a lake

of mist on the valley floor, sky
white with early winter.

We sit by an outside fire, eat, drink wine,
talk of the past and of poetry.

As we part – you to fly
twelve thousand miles, I

to walk the ridge path to my cabin –
I think of Li Po's farewell to Meng Hao-Jan,

'Nothing left but a river
flowing on the borders of heaven.'

Wrens at Nightfall

I don't know where they come from
those fluttering wrens at nightfall
visiting the dying peach tree; half
bird, half
leaf or butterfly, rising high against the white
sky then falling back as if
there's something, after all, they can't
ever quite let go of.

THE MAGPIE

Age, and the deaths, and the ghosts
—John Berryman, 'He Resigns'

Christmas Eve. She having finished
her renovations in the cabin, we went down
to spend the night there, sit out
on the old wooden deck to see
what stars we could through the thickening cloud.
Our neighbour down the slope, where the creek rises,
had lit a fire in the middle of his field – a dangerous thing
to do, I would have said, and probably illegal too –
but we watched it grow, a true bonfire, heard his children
playing off in the dark around it, and I found myself
remembering the fires of my childhood
and the joy and magic of them, and for a time the night
became a throwback to a lost world, a light
rain coming and going, assuring the fire wouldn't catch.

We woke at seven, drank coffee, ate
some of the cake she'd made, then received a call
to say my ex-partner, with whom things had not ended well,
had died, and a crowd of regrets I'd been holding at bay
stirred from their places, which might almost explain
why two hours later, in the garden, digging out
potatoes for our Christmas meal, I fell
and, rather than rising, chose to lie
staring at the empty sky
until she came and righted me.

I rested, then, no harm done, and by noon
was in the cabin, working,
when out of nowhere a young man
in sandals and swamp-stained shorts
appeared from the bottom of the paddock, so
seemingly at home you'd think he owned the place.
I asked if I could help him – trying
to contain my alarm – and, when he stopped
and looked at me as if surprised to see *me* there,
explained this was not public land.
All he said was that there'd been
'a situation', gesturing
to the creek below, then turned
and went the way he'd come, down
through the middle gate, then turning right, vanishing
into the clump of ti-tree there – a lost
or homeless man, I've subsequently thought,
and felt bad for him
though for a time I wondered if I'd seen a ghost.

That evening, just
before our meal, there was
a second call, and
anger, recrimination, such wild pain
as one hopes never to hear again.
We ate at last in silence, there being
so little that could be easily said,
and shortly after went to bed.

Next morning, Boxing Day, a neighbour stopping by
to return a saw he'd borrowed, we talked, at the gate,
a good half hour or more

and when we came back
found a magpie had entered through an open door
and was walking so
slowly and
priest-like through the house
I could almost imagine him
carrying an invisible *encensoir*,
wafting carefully
into every room
the scent of rosemary or sandalwood
or myrrh.

More

the glow of the last tomatoes
on their leafless vines
against the dark soil of the garden bed
the lustre of the new grass
after this afternoon's rain – some
days the light might almost be enough
though if you asked me what more I could want
that would be it, more

Sorting Things Out

each day
like this
the checking of the garden beds,
straightening of stakes and borders,
harvesting whatever's ready

arranging for the driveway
gate to be repaired,
the east side of the house to be repainted
before the winter rains

pausing to hear the treecreeper
or the butcherbird

feeding the animals

checking the mail,
listening to news,
writing to friends,

breaking bread,
drinking wine with the living

sorting it all out
peace by peace

the four horsemen, the molten chariot, the ending of time

Black Cockatoos

ed è subito sera
—Salvatore Quasimodo

Day after day lately I've seen them
down in the stringybarks, barely
fifty metres from me,
today one, I'd swear,
with a flash of red in his tail, clambering
from tree to tree, tumbling from one
branch to the branch below
as if drunk, but that's their way

I feel
they follow me – how could that be? – from
year to year, as if they've got
some message for me
though they seem
in no great hurry to deliver it

Anyway, they were there, as I said, today,
a half hour or so, then flew away

and suddenly it was evening

FROM *Open House* 2015

A PLACE ON EARTH

A young boy
is sitting by a fire
on the edge of the desert. There's a car
through the scrub behind him
pulled off to the side of the long dirt road
and a tent close by with his father in it, sleeping
already. It is late evening, nine or ten,
and he's long ago eaten: toast, baked
beans on a tin plate, burnt potatoes, tea.
1964 perhaps, or '63:
it doesn't matter what year.
He is sitting by the fire, stoked
earlier so that now it's burned back to the ancient
fire-gutted log he found and dragged there
before the sun set – burned back
so that, now the log is deep alight,
he can see a world in it: sees falling towers, forgotten
Alexandrias and Babylons,
the night markets of Wúzhōu, Rangoon, Hong Kong,
sees Siegfried and the *Götterdämmerung*,
sees a huge, blood-orange sun
setting over the burnt, black
hills around him,
autos-da-fé, charred ruins, faces
staring from the flame
so beautiful they seem to scorch him,

sees the bombing and the burning of Dresden,
bodies in fiery graves, wild
midnight *carnevales*, sees
Moon-men and Sun-men in corroboree,
sees hearth-fires and bonfires and beacon-fires,
Etnas in their scoriac flows,
townspeople and villagers fleeing,
docks and homes and factories alight,
sees battered galleons, masts
collapsing, armadas blazing on the sea, radiant
sunrise breaking from the glowing embers
as if out of a phoenix nest.

Something
rustles in the ti-tree, a
wallaby perhaps, night bird or
wild dog drawn by the fire,
and he looks up from his dreaming, sees the huge
darkness of the night and the vast
canopy of unknown, unnameable stars,
a night so infinite, this night,
it will never leave him.
Time and again he will look up
– for sixty or for seventy years, luck holding – and it
will always be there: before him
the fire, behind him
his father sleeping, that something
rustling in the undergrowth,
and about him the galaxies turning, the still
point of his being,
a place on Earth,
gift beyond measure.

The Thick of It

I was standing there, washing up and
thinking about Baudelaire, how one might
give one's soul
to be able to write so well
but then the dog came down
to lap at his water bowl and
sleep on the armchair
and on some obscure
impulse I went out
into the night air, for the
thick of it, the
hum of life everywhere – looked
at the stars, the
insects
swarming about the back-door lamp, and
coming in, stepped over first a
cockroach then a
slug, leading its
small family somewhere.

How can we
be so arrogant, to think that our
souls are worth so much?

Poem

Since I have come upstairs
on all fours to greet him, the dog,
for such is his wont,
licks first the top of my head and then my left ear, just as,
if he can catch me, he'll
lick any cracked or wounded skin as I
get up in the morning – it's
nothing that I can't wash off
and probably helps
heal some other, more ancient hurt, or
balms it.

It is
a warm spring day. The smell
of each of us
rises gently into the ether, yours
of lemons and wood-smoke, summer flowers, his
of grass and dust and beloved
blanket, mine – for such
is my own
ancient wont –
of you.

No Poem for Weeks Now

No poem for weeks now, I don't know why – the
flood of things – then suddenly, tonight, just
after 1 am,
from the other end of the house, you
singing under your breath, so
quietly that, through the rain, the
sound of the heater, trucks
on the highway changing gear, I can
barely hear but
do and
close my eyes, breathe
outward, slowly, a breath it
seems I have held for years.

WINTER LONGING POEM

Though I leave all the doors
and windows open
my longing for you
will not leave this house.

The Ten Towns Down

Those sounds again, each night,
over and over as the dark unfolds, great
punchings and shudderings of air, as if
squadrons of dragons were taking flight,

such screechings and clangings as might attest
the closing of the seven gates of Hell,
thunderings, like the stampede
of a thousand wilderbeest

or moanings, like the lonely
calvings of a glacier – but no, it's only
the coal train from Lithgow
as it crests the range, begins the slow

descent towards Sydney, hauls
its thousand tonnes of cold black fire
through Katoomba, Leura, Wentworth Falls
and our dreams with them, all the ten towns down.

Night Rain II

Night rain
washing the mountains again
reminding us all of the sea we can't have,
just like the sea does,
just like the sea.

September

Straight
from the flight
it's as if my sight is hypersensitised, flooded
by the thick late-summer light, the figs
gravid on the boughs, grapes
almost over-ready, the lavender
alive with bees.
In the dark kitchen, a small
mountain of fresh-picked tomatoes
glows in a wicker basket, and Nona,
telling me about the season,
runs her fingers through a bowl
of just-husked beans
to show me how fat they are, each one
a living gemstone, agate
veined with purple. There's frozen spinach too,
Maria says, we have to eat
to make way for the rest, and an abundance
of pale green peppers
ready for roasting.
Eight hours later, in
bed at last, your breasts
and belly
are firm fruit in my hands,
your back, your neck, your shoulders
taste of sun.

Swallows

4 pm, the hour
of the hundred swallows,
skimming the sky-coloured pool.

How hard
to write the simplest things,
these sabre-sharp wings
severing words from their stems.

Pears

It's the fourth of July in Australia
but still the third here, the night hot
and the full moon rising over Nova Vas;
she is lying back in the deckchair
trying to work out her new mobile phone
and I'm inspecting the ruins of my
backpack, caught in airport machinery
at Frankfurt or Helsinki, hardly
a problem, now I think about it,
given the mess I've just flown above,
the shelling of innocent civilians,
the bombs in the crowded markets,
asylum boats foundering in the Indian Ocean,
whales dying from explosive harpoons,
elephants falling to their knees
shot for their tusks, the cattle
and the sheep filed to their
deaths in the great Satanic
Mills of the slaughterhouses, and suddenly
Emiliano comes up, with a
basket of pears, maybe fifty
or sixty of them, all perfect, each
the size of young child's fist,
wanting us just to see them, I guess, how
beautiful they are, with the first
russet blush of summer on them, and I
take one as he leaves, as he
wants me to, walk
over to the balcony wall

and stand there, eating it, stare
out at the distant lights of the villages,
making no sense of anything,
engulfed in mystery.

Jennifer's Mound

'It was that time again: almost out of meat and
seven pigs fattening at an alarming rate. A house meeting
and it was decided, Jennifer it would have to be, the
oldest and largest, or Two-spot, the next in size, though it
had been
such a hassle to get the last one down the mountain for the
killing
we decided we would try to do it here – or
get it done, if Steve would come up from Radiance, a gentle
giant of a guy when he wasn't overdoing acid, a
butcher's son, and excellent with a gun
since that's the way I wanted it, quick and
painless; as the cook I guess it was my say.
And that's how it was, standing a little back
from the middle of the kitchen door, out of sight's way,
taking aim at Jenny at the centre of the yard
on the mound of dirt and gravel someone
had brought there for something they'd
never got around to, well before I came,
now all grown over with couch grass and
dandelion and dock, which for some reason
the pigs had decided they'd rather
doze upon than crop.
One
rifle shot and a
second of shock and she was down, as
clean as you could have wished it, dead
before she hit the ground. I should
have moved the others out

if I'd have thought of it, but didn't. We
loaded her onto a cart – much squealing then – and
took her round the front, where Steve strung her up
on the post-frame over the gate he reckoned
must have been used for that purpose before,
bled her, slit her open, gathered her guts
in an old washing tub, cleaned her and cut her up, the rest
of them eerily silent now, huddled against the far fence
on the other side of the house.

'It's not that but the next morning I'm thinking about:
getting up at 5 am to make coffee in the strange
quiet and the mist and, looking out,
seeing them there, all six, lying
on the mound like ghostly sentinels, their grief
as pervasive as the mist itself. They kept it up for days
and afterward migrated to the far side of the shed.

'We ate her, as you have to do, out of respect, and then – it
was only weeks – I said, knowing
it was probably the end of me there, I said
That's it. I'm never cooking meat again.'

Witness

You're spared, for
something, as
witness. Not
knowing what
will be of help. No
thought to
who might hear. That
vineyard there – the long
rectangle of
striated green – planted
with money from the
dictator; that
story you heard
yesterday
about the young
poet in Buchenwald
who could do nothing after
but drink and
wander; this bright
morning with its melon and
peaches
warm from the sun; the
panic
in the young cow's eye; you
cannot not
utter you must
say, and say.

In the Kingdom of Shadows

In the back lanes and alleyways
a few late humans are scuttling off
abandoned by their bicycles
but don't worry, they

are diurnal, if we
don't frighten them
they will flow eventually over us
like slow, tainted light.

In the kingdom of shadows,
in the march of the middle night,
the last embers of the day gone out,
the puppets are lost in their stupors of desire.

In the kingdom of shadows, world without end,
slugs traverse the prairies of the soul,
mice enter the pure land,
cockroaches conquer the valleys of death.

In the kingdom of shadows, dominion
of cats and sugar gliders,
moths are mastering the constellations, spiders
whispering their histories to the stars.

Spiders About the House

Up here it's funnel-web country,
build a house and it draws them around,
every basement a Chartres or a Coventry,
every low window a trawling-ground:
garden with gloves on, take care
when you're under the deck,
touch a trip-wire and you summon them,
move a log too quickly
and one might leap at your neck.
They come up through the floorboards
to escape the wet, roam widely in springtime
looking for a mate, can get aggressive
when whatever passes for their blood is up.
I don't like to kill anyone, deadly or not,
but I draw a line at my thresholds:
any such neighbour that crosses them
might be neighbour no more.
Perhaps the best that you can say
is that funnel-webs keep red-backs away,
though very few others: certainly not the wolf spiders
who riddle our lawn with their burrows
and can be seen out hunting at night,
their emerald eyes glinting in torchlight,
or the St Andrew's Cross, with their great wide
web outside the back door, my
almost favourite, so
perfect the X they make of themselves, right
at the centre, like men spread-
eagled in the middle of their being

or ski jumpers at the top of their flight, second only
to the mystic orb spider whose intricate tracery
between the wormwood and the lemon tree
is such a metaphor for poetry.
And yet there are more – the daddy-long-legs, say,
supposedly most poisonous of all
were he ever able to get fangs through skin
or the tiny, tentative swimmer I found in
the bathroom sink last winter, who stayed
three days or so, savouring the splash
of surf, the waves, thirsty beyond measure
for something I suspect there is no measuring,
or those other two, internal and, I guess, my
point in writing this: the one
whose web you see only on the MRI, the neat
bundles of her victims at C2 or 3 (you
never see the spider herself, but feel her, late at night,
testing the guy-ropes, patrolling
the trip-wires, tugging here and there where
something on a nerve needs tightening), and
this last one, stranger still,
whose web's his life itself: damaged
and torn, repaired a hundred times, ob-
ssessive beyond imagining, he'll
lumber out at almost any trouble or
excitement in his neighbourhood,
wrap it clumsily in a
cocoon of words, as if he thought it could
be kept, or understood.

Eight Mile

In the house on the ridge
at the Eight Mile, on the old verandah,
people are talking
late into the night,
about suffering and memory, history, loss,
the comings and the goings of love,
the rights of the living and the dead.
A three-quarter moon
rises and lingers overhead
and is slowly covered by cloud;
wind picks up and then calms.
Unnoticed, a young possum
sits a long while in a tree-fork, watching.

Someone stands, goes inside,
comes back with another bottle.

The sky clears.
The moon
shines down again.
Somewhere in the trees below
a night bird swoops, catches something,
takes it away.

Tips of cigarettes
glow in the dark.

The talk continues.

A Call from Mandelstam

... Osip
Mandelstam that is, great
Russian poet, died
in exile in Siberia, 1938: I'm
standing in the kitchen, 11 pm, doing
the last of the washing-up, staring
out through the window
at first at the night's great blackness, then
at the delicately scalloped underwing
of a snow-white moth
almost as big as the palm of my hand
crawling slowly over the upper pane, the
intricate articulation of the legs, the
albino redness of the eyes, when I get
this sudden urge for *poetry*,
so strong it's like an addict's doubling.
I don't drop everything, of course, since
everything is nearly done,
but rinse the last pot and put it on the rack, drain
the water, dry my hands, then
glancing back at the window as if
the moth might just have a clue for me
go in to the bookcase in the living room
where we've put almost all of the poetry,
but whatever it is that is calling me
certainly isn't there. It isn't
Yeats, it isn't Pound, it isn't John Clare,
isn't Lorca, isn't Miłosz, isn't Strand,
isn't James Baxter, isn't Merwin, isn't Bly, shelf

after shelf, nearly a thousand books, and nothing
seems to be reaching me, nothing responds. I
turn to the Australians but it's the same thing again,
not Wright, not Hope, not Adamson, not J.S. Harry – even
my beloved Chinese are not helping me tonight,
not Tu Fu, not Wang Wei, not Li Po, not Po Chű-I,
though in frustration I'm about to take my ancient
Penguin Book of Chinese Verse when I remember, without
much hope or enthusiasm, the musty set
of *Modern European Poets*
at ground-level under the ornaments on the
far side of the room, but it's not Pavese, not Cendrars,
not Blok, not Yevtushenko, not Celan, so much
horror, so much sadness there, yet the wanting
is almost an aching in my belly now;
then, just as I'm about to stand, my eye
catches the spine of Osip Mandelstam and something
draws my hand almost despite itself. I reflect
a little guiltily that I remember almost nothing about him, have
never even opened the book, yellow
and dog-eared as this copy is, so
I take it – what else to do? – and go upstairs, sit
on the edge of the bed, pull
off my shoes and
socks and
open it at random,
and there it is, page 64, poem one hundred and
twenty-seven: *'For life'*, it says, *'for life*
and care,
I'll give up everything.
A kitchen match could keep me warm.'

Ninox strenua

Ninox strenua, the Powerful Owls, stand
sixty centimetres tall and have wingspans
of almost one hundred and fifty, 'defend'
a territory of up to fifteen hundred hectares
though hunt much wider. Have beaks
tough as boltcutters, mate for life, live
on a diet of ring-tailed possum and sweet
sugar glider, are endangered and rarely seen
though their two-note call is familiar
to anyone who listens to the bush at night.
In our catchment there's at least one breeding pair,
working its way as the months pass
anti-clockwise over an area twenty by
twenty kilometres – four hundred square.
The local wildlife rescue service
will not release young possums into the scrub
at any time near the full moon and until
they've checked the raptor's whereabouts.
Ninox strenua are rumoured to kill
up to thirty ring-tailed possums each per night, and, almost
human in their wastefulness,
eat only the brain.

FREIGHT

A hot night,
no sign of the promised storm.
You argue with your parents
long distance – that
bloody priest again – and then
go out to the deck
to watch the quarter moon
ride the clouds westward.
So much
still left unsaid – the bed
so full of ghosts
we hold each other
waiting for sleep to blanket them.

At 3 am – your breathing
calm and deeper now – something
triggers the porch light
and I hear the scream
of some small creature
cut suddenly off: just
that, no
wing-sound, no
scuttering of cat

and then, five
minutes later, the long
slow ache of a freight train,
and the starting rain.

Carmen 193

All day the poet writes
about the wondrous creatures of the world,
the beasts, the fishes and the birds,
their gracefulness, their speed, their flight,
then, wonder typed and safely filed,
wonders which of them to eat tonight.

Captain Hunter and the Petrels

Tuesday the 12th of February and I've gone to see Andrew, picked
up a few things from the bookshop on the way – two
novels since I'm in that mood, a book
of paintings of Australian birds and a CD of Gurrumul Yunupingu
whose voice haunted me so much a year ago – then
gone to the dentist, the second time in two days,
and come home numb-jawed to read the news of how
an elderly Catholic priest with dementia has been fined
for biting the ear off another
in a fight over a parking spot. In
the bird book there's a story of how, in 1790, shipwrecked
John Hunter, the crew of the *Sirius* and Norfolk Island's five
hundred inhabitants (mostly prisoners) avoided starvation by eating
one hundred and seventy thousand of its nesting petrels. A
rescue ship arrived in August, but the petrel – named
'Providence' accordingly (from *providore*) –
has never recovered; the only image we have of it
was drawn by Captain Hunter himself
as his victim was on her way to the cooking pot. The book
has also several illustrations of the Mountain Lowry
and as I read about the petrels I was thinking
of the bird that hit the study window yesterday – how
we heard the *thunk* from the kitchen
just as the rain began, and went in
to find the smudge-mark on the pane and the oh-
so-beautiful lowry lying on the grass below – a
'heart break', as Teja might have said – so
still I could not imagine that he wasn't dead, but she
saw movement and ran down

and came back holding him closely to her chest
and within two minutes he had woken and
suddenly flown, leaving only, on the lawn, a single
green-blue feather, such as John Hunter might have drawn.
A poem is a place where you can bring things together, you
don't have to know why. The mad and the bad, the
gentle and the dead, toothache and heartache
and the ache and quandary of history. We are all
creatures trembling under the sun of witness (or
is it rain?); some of us, for reasons it would be hard to explain,
trying to catch the strange, sad music of it,
on the days we can hear it,
before it disappears again.

How to Ride a Horse

Once the hair was removed, the tanners would bate the material by pounding dung into the skin, or soaking the skin in a solution of animal brains.
—Wikipedia, entry on 'Tanning'

To ride a live horse, it must be said,
you must first have a dead one,
which you have had *flayed*
to remove the *skin* or *hide*, and which then –
with the aid of an essence of oak-tree or
a sequence, less expensively,
of urine, faeces and animals' brains –
you've had *cured* or *tanned*
before, dried and beaten to soften it,
you've had it cut into various lengths and shapes
for the saddle, the reins, the straps,
and the hat, belt and boots
that a rider wears (their wallet, their whip, their
watchband, their crop), the rest
of the carcase having long been consigned
to the makers of dog-food and glue.

As for the second, the living horse,
it must be *broken*, unless of course
it has been *bred in captivity*, when it may be deemed
to have been broken from the start. Saddled,
with the bit and the reins in place,
it can then be mounted and (the dead
horse on the living's back) gently

goaded by the rider's ankles, its mouth
pulled firmly to the left or right,
made to follow any track a rider might.
Stroked, occasionally, and brushed,
stalled, watered, given hay – *loved*,
as riders are wont to say – until such time
as it becomes a dead horse (etc.),
it should be of service indefinitely. (You may,
in the above, care, where
appropriate, to substitute
'dead cow' for 'dead horse'.)

Now to talk about fences …

The Gate

What are they after, those huge dogs
we see sometimes at the street gate
or through one of the boundary fences, emerging
from the dusk, the scrub, suddenly *there*,
then gone before you can call anyone
or tell for certain what breed they are, Bull-
mastiff, you'd think, though crossed
with Doberman or Arab or Great Dane? Someone's
pig-hunting dogs maybe, let loose
or just got free, roaming with impunity,
and we worry for the sheep, the ducks, the rabbits, our own
farm dog or any other creature sheltering here, waking at night
to listen for anything unusual, hair raised
at any sound of a squall, checking each morning
to make sure all are there. You see them
once or twice in a week sometimes, then maybe
just once in a month or so, but it can be much longer, and you forget
about telling the Council, raising the fences, asking the vet
for what she might know of them, then look up
and suddenly they are there again, tight
browed, thick jowled, black eyed, the dark
forest behind them, staring from the gate.

Another Page from the Book of Everything

with the error so entrenched that we'll never root it out
with all the human evils and the good that tracks them
    like gulls following a ship at sea
with all the seas and the swelling oceans, the creeks and
    pools and rivers that run down to them
the Seine and the Parramatta, the Arno, the Mara
    with its swift dark current and its wooden mills,
    the Sava with its freight of bodies just shot or
    throats cut at the waterside
with the company of poets whispering their secret graft
    like old men showing each other
    their gemstones on the Ponte Vecchio
with the Ponte Vecchio, the Pont Neuf, the Rialto, the Harbour Bridge
    and the sludge that gropes under them,
    taking Florence and Paris and Sydney to their separate inseparate seas
with the intolerable and hideous weight of them
    and their paradoxical lightness, the girders and the steeples
with their infinite mysteries,
    their intricate filigrees of rust
with the human Gargantuas eating their way
    through all of the flocks of the earth,
    each day in each person
    seventeen kinds of death
with the beasts themselves caged or in pasture or transport trucks,
with their soft muzzles, their large innocent eyes,
    the pale whisps of their breath in the dawn fields
    or by gas station lights at midnight
with the vast manscapes and the roads that lead to them
    severing and dividing the indivisible (O fields of illusion!)

with the wombat-holes by the highway at Lake George
    and the pomegranates overhanging the old road to Tressan,
    we humans stumbling about
    so dangerous in our guilt and loneliness
with the cockatoos circling and the water
    flowing into the dam, my neighbour Franklin coming out
    with his big tin of birdseed,
    pouring it into the white plastic bowl, another
lightness with its myriad strange messages, another
day with its hands wide open
another page from the book of everything

Report from Blue Mountains

1

My *Echium*, exotic that it is,
has collapsed under the weight of its own blossoming.
This afternoon, while I tried to string it,
the sun slipped behind a bank of cloud
and the first fat drops of a heavy shower fell.
As I climbed the steps to the back verandah, the dog following,
I saw a tiny beetle on the handrail
hesitate and turn, as if deciding to make for home.
The rain, as I sat in the doorway, thundered on the roof, like wonder,
halting us all.

2

It is spring in the mountains, uncertain spring.
One day it hails and the temperature drops,
the next it is windy and thirty degrees.
Plants bolt upward and then stop, as if thinking they have come too far.
The grass is thick and wild, full of dandelions, scotch thistle, rogue
poppies, dock.
This morning I found myself longing for a country
where no one understands me.
Tonight a large moth has been keeping me company,
dusting my shoulders with her yellow wings.

Silent Night

Christmas Eve, and the dogs are exchanging
season's greetings over the backblocks,
the smell of a barbeque over the fence
filling the air with sacrifice,
the ritual about to commence,
the festival of gluttony and slaughter,
cooks stuffing their turkeys,
children clustering about the Christmas tree
like ants at sugar water.

All day the lists and anxiety,
the rudeness at the checkouts,
the anger in the parking lots,
the loneliness in shuttered houses,
the ragged nativities on the lawns,
police busy and the highways choked,
suicides preparing their Stilnox,
paramedics checking their stocks
of oxygen, adrenalin, morphine.

Christmas Eve, and the long-distance phone calls,
the Bloody Marys, the *Glühwein*, the priests
and ministers sharpening their prayers, hosts
scraping and salting their grill-plates,
checking their bar fridge, their prawns on ice,
the Queen delivering her annual message,
pleading for peace and family,
regretting that her husband, in hospital for a stent,
won't be presiding over this year's hunt.

Christmas Eve, and all through the house
the tension, the expectation, the wonder.
Soon the children will be fed.
Soon they will be put to bed.
Soon the carols will begin
for a world redeemed of sin:
Silent night, crystal night …
Soon the tables will be set.
Soon the ovens will be lit.

'Unto us
a child is born,
unto us a Son is given',
and from the squalor of the feedlots,
the horror of the holding yards,
the abject terror of the abattoirs,
under mute, indifferent stars,
unthought, unvoiced, ungiven,
the cows, the sheep, the geese look on.

Reading to the Sheep

It is a cold afternoon in early winter and my wife
is reading to the sheep the first departmental seminar paper
from her doctoral thesis while unbeknownst to her
I watch through the kitchen window. She is wearing
her heavy winter jacket, and the sheep
in their thickening coats
are chewing on the already-stripped stalks of the rampant mint
and what is left of the autumn grass around the potato bed.
The thesis is on the grief of animals and she is reading
about the mourning of chickens for their mates,
about the grief of calves for their mothers, mothers for their stolen
calves,
about huge elephants in the Kenyan dusk
turning over and over the bones of their dead,
she is reading about birds
placing branches over the bodies of their companions,
and about how, knowing that they did not know, the Lord
of some people or another – maybe it was ours –
sent crows to teach them due
reverence and rites for the departed,[4]
she is reading about ants, carrying away
so carefully the bodies of their fellows,
she is reading about dogs
starving themselves after the loss of their loved ones,
about dolphins holding, at the surface of the water, their dying friends,

about macaque mothers carrying their infants
for months after the last breath has left them.

Now and again, when she pauses, lost
in the incipience of her own sorrow perhaps,
or just asking for breath,
one or another of the two sheep comes to her
in the sad May twilight
and with the top of his head, where
the horns have not so long ago been sawn away,
nudges her hand
as if to comfort her,
or perhaps only to ask her to turn a page.

The light thickens, and a wind picks up. Ducks
settle about her and the sheep
rest at her feet. Night
turns into day, then night, then day again.
Rain comes and goes. The seminar passes. Spring
turns into early summer, drifts on towards autumn.
The sheep rise, stretch, graze, return,
leaves pile around them and are blown
away by the winds of another winter.
Your hair
turns grey – look at it! – and a million lines
come to the backs of your hands.
You find this poem.
She is still reading.

Each Other's Tongue

Coming out before bed
to watch the moonlight from the deck
I hear a pump still working
and going down to turn it off
suddenly can see the moon properly
its rays reaching from horizon to horizon
playing on a receding edge of cloud
and on the winter grass
and on the backs of the sheep
who to my surprise are still up, watching

One comes over
and I scratch his neck
deep under the thickening wool,
bending over
to catch his hot breath on my cheek
and together we murmur about moonlight,
for one brief moment
understanding each other's tongue

FROM *The Balcony* 2008

WAIT

During the night the orb
spider has been repairing her huge
web above the entryway.
She has been there for over a year now
and almost every day her work is damaged.
Sometimes the heart grows so large
it floods the body.
Sometimes it is no bigger than a nut.
Sometimes the dark creeps in
and it seems that it will never go away.
A great deal that is lost is findable.
Much that seems dead
is not at dead at all.
Much that is obvious
needs to be said
again and again.

The Balcony

I

Straight from the airport and already, in two days,
she has taken my virginity in more ways
than I can count. She is
outside on the balcony, translating poetry again,
carrying words
from one language to the other, bribing
the border-guards, arguing with the grammarians,
pulling the wool
over the eyes of the lexicographers.
I go out
and kiss her, so long this time
that it gets dark
and the street clears of traffic.
When I open my eyes
the moonlight almost blinds me.
She is
writing a message
with her tongue on my neck
in a language I don't understand,
there are birds
nesting in my hair,
my skin
is singing
a wild, untranslatable *jubilate*.

2

The flying foxes are screeching in the trees outside the window.
They are angry and jealous and want us to stop.
We have been making love
for almost eighteen hours, they say,
and they are afraid for their reputation. We must
love to rule, no
moaning like this in the bedroom, no making
the floor-boards creak, no
sudden, explosive cries, no
comings without goings – only
launchings out from the balcony, ridings
on the evening thermals, glidings,
fruit-ward, arms
extended, against
the huge night sky.

3

She is
riding me, facing
away,
and I am
deep inside her.
The moles
and freckles
on her back
are an unknown constellation.
On the other side
of the universe – much
too far away
and far

too dark to see –
there are
her perfect breasts,
her face,
her closed eyes.

4

We are sitting on a beach at night
and there is a storm out to sea. The lightning
illuminates the headland
with a regular, sudden halo
then races off, horizontally, for South America.
In the dark it leaves behind
the white
crests hasten towards us
wave after wave
as if there were almost no time left
as if there were almost
no time at all
and they were so desperate to touch us.

5

10 pm
on a midsummer evening
and again
we start to kiss on the balcony.
Someone on the street
whistles
and a small group gathers.
There are cat-calls, cheers, mock applause,

someone else
arrives in a taxi,
a bus
pulls up
in the middle of traffic
with all of its windows open.
After a while
the crowd
stops jeering. People
watch on in utter silence.
When we look up
no one is there,
the leaves
have fallen from the trees,
the koels
and swallows have departed,
it is almost winter.

A Different Life

The castle
leans in through the roof.
Someone has plastered
directly under the thatch.
Small pieces have been falling
for a hundred years.

Underwear
dries slowly on the line.
Now and again
a child's voice
rises from the yard.
All day the swallows
scythe the blue air.

What do you want from a poem?

The truth?

In my other life
I knew so much.

LANGUAGE

We talk all night
peeling back the layers.
Later it seems
not even the skin comes between us.
In the morning
I watch you put it all on again,
the language,
the past,
the mind's clothes as well as the body's.
You step out onto the street
and the street catches you,
but the street knows only the half of it.
Pale, soft fruit. Odour of dusk.

Starlight

The old dog in the lumber yard
whimpers in his sleep.
A man walks down
Station Street in the rain.

Under the bandstand
in the Blackheath Public Gardens
a cicada stirs
fooled by some ghost of the day.

In the dark we are
eating each other,
tearing, smelling, entering
with fingers, memory, desire,

there are
worms in our hair,
roots in our flesh,
our tongues taste starlight.

Major's Creek

Flash of kingfisher green
across the dirt road
old she-oak
amid a million gums
platypus water

what point in becoming
when we don't know where we are?

The Ibex

My panther is active tonight,
hungry, intent,
nobody's business but her own

not content
to leave me
gutted by moonlight,
I must be
her lair-thing,
her skin-to-lie-on,
her gnawed bone.

Thinking Like Pigeons

The dust is okay
dust I know

and the sunlight
and the boredom
the wandering about
over the dirt and the grass and the pavement
these things I know well enough too

I'm as sick of the puffers
and the pouters as anyone

and being chased
by dogs and children
the crowding
around the shit-covered fountain
the pecking about
for things that people throw to you
avoiding the cats
seem to be things
all of us know in our bones

but the settling sounds
in the eaves at dusk
that ease on the roof-tiles
that drifting
high over the square
with the sunlight breaking
into a thousand

arrows over your wings
that sudden lifting
and soaring over the campanile
that banking towards the sea

ah …

Balkan

She's still at the age
where she thinks that she's immortal,
smokes too much,
drives far too fast,
has the patience
of spilt quicksilver,
can drink almost anyone under the table,
claims that she has
a special dispensation from God,
maybe because she met the Pope once,
more likely because she's seen some things
and knows how to farm a secret;
has a revolver in her wardrobe,
a fetish for
knocking into people on the street,
hates, like she loves, unconditionally,
always gets what she wants,
wants me.

Gift

After we had paid the singer,
and the guests had gone
and we had cleared away the food and the glasses,
I went outside again
and the moon, which had been so high over the dancers,
was already four times larger
and even more full,
setting over the hills to the west,
sharpening the outline of the pines,
making the ridges shimmer,
and I thought of it shining
on the other side, beyond Isola, a long
silver path on the rippled water,
and of the silent ships out there
some of them with their lights still burning,
and of the sailors on watch,
smoking, and drinking quietly into the night,
and of what they might be thinking,
and I realised that, undeserved
and against all odds,
something extraordinary had come upon me, a great
happiness,
and for once I didn't question it,
didn't ask why.

The Cricket

There is a cricket
loose in the house,
in the cantina, most likely, or
hallway somewhere, ridden in
in the last basket of eggplants or
bucket of dusty tomatoes,
its huge, blue-velvet spasms of sound
breaking out just as we have put the
dinner-things away,
filling the cantina night
like slow domestic lightning,
turning the bathroom and hallway, the
kitchen and the laundry and the
drying-room
into a sudden forest or
trellised field under starlight
as if the potatoes and tomatoes and the
fresh-picked beans in the cantina dark
were still lying
ten inches down
in the warm earth under the midsummer moon
or hanging under silver-shadowed
night-breeze-shifted leaves,
not in a plastic milk-crate by the wine vat
or a brown paper bag among the
empty oil bottles and still-to-be-mended hose.

It is
almost impossible to find it: every time
we make a move in what we
think is its direction it
stops completely, will not start again
until we have convinced it we have
given up and gone away, like deer
no longer foraging in a cornfield
or pigs
no longer rooting in the deep cantina grass – not
humans
wandering back to their television
and their glasses of wine or,
as we really do,
standing, hearts racing, by the
part-opened hallway door
secretly praying for the next
outbreak of shock-blue sound, hoping
to trick its uncanny early-warning system long enough
to track the voice-line, find
the source of this
mystical thunder-crystal of song that, when at last, by
accident we do so
almost a half-hour later
in a crack by the doorjamb
proves to be – this
black and shining
onyx-shard, this
feral poet, this
bellowing sliver of midnight – just
one centimetre long.

DAMAGE

Sometimes I think that just through existing
one creates damage and disappointment,
and that love keeps us open, that
long, beautiful wound

that one has the choice
to do as little as one can
but that even that will not change one's allotted portion
of sadness and destruction – that it will be there
whatever one does to avoid it
and that the challenge is not to escape it,
try as of course we must,
but to think of life differently, as something
other than how we thought it was

No matter how careful one attempts to be
there is always greater care to be taken

as we avoid one thing
another will always happen

and the hermit's solution is no solution at all
simply a re-framing of the problem
a not recognising, a failure to see
how the immense weight of being
is always shifting away from itself
and how the damage is also the gap
between what we are
and what we have been thinking that we could be

and that this is the price of becoming
if that is what we want to do –

not to be sought or welcomed
but to be known and sometimes forgiven

and that pain and error and regret are a
kind of light in themselves, showing a path
one can never see by holding oneself or
any of them at bay

In the dark one can sometimes see
so much more clearly than in the day.

The Magician[5]

1 *Levitation*

From the calm with which the smiling magician
raises the apparently-sleeping woman from the ground
using only the intentness of his gaze
and an almost-imperceptible shifting of his fingers
then takes the shining silver hoop
and moves it with such loving care
all the way along her silk-clad body
from the tips of her feet to the last
strand of her tumbled, golden hair,
to show that no trick has been used, no hand or
hidden strings have touched her, you would almost think
people could see her, almost swear
that no one could tell
it's been six years since she was there.

2 *Sawing a Woman in Half*

Practice makes perfect, and at last
you can do it in the full light of day
sanguine and almost bloodless,
the way the great magician taught you,
inserting the blade into the groove,
moving it slowly through the stomach and spine,
turning the half-boxes outward
to show the neatness of the cut, the feet
protruding from the one, the bitter smile
still accusing you from the other,
then, later, empty-handed, limping off – their cold applause

barely disguising their fascination and disdain –
wondering when someone will hand you back the saw
for the house, the bank account, the car.

3 *Leaving Everything Standing*

You've seen it, surely, in some old movie on TV,
one of those classic party tricks
that almost never comes off, the dapper guy
in the half-tux taking the edge of the table-cloth
while all the dinner-guests are sitting there
before full plates and glasses, candles, bowls of fruit, and
whipping it away so deftly that they barely notice, leaving
everything still standing, the wine unspilt, the soup
still steaming in the bowls, the conversation
continuing without pause – it must
be the dream of every escape artist, to do it
without interruption, without spillage, without fuss, the party
still in full swing, the wife and the guests
still happy: no damage, no anger, no disgust.

4 *Making the Self Disappear*

At last he comes, our magician,
to the hardest trick of all.
He tries it with love.
He tries it with courage.
He tries it with alcohol.

He drives to the edge
a dozen times
hoping the moment might have come

but something always stops him,
something always drives him home.

At last he tries a heart attack
but even the body fights back.
What would take most people
just one or two
takes the Magician nine

each time
a little more
slipping from view,
each time a little closer
to the final *legerdemain*.

The toughest thing
when the disappearer is you:
knowing
that the heart that does it
has to go too.

No Point in Staying Up Longer

No point in staying up longer,
thoughts all sad and astray,
the Six Sisters sound asleep long ago,
and the seventh away,
Orion gone off with his hounds somewhere
and the Great Bear sleeping,
Castor and Pollux and Aldebaran
so far up in the mountains now
dream-chasing
no one is calling them home.

Boria

Winter
and the Boria come full force
clubbing and clubbing at the village
all night and into the morning,
shaking the doors and windows
like a man whose wife has locked him out
or a soldier come home to find no one,
only a lean, angry dog in the neighbours' yard
howling for no reason,
tearing at anything not tied down.

Stoop

She stoops
and ushers the cockroach outside,
the cockroach, or the spider, the slug, the moth, no matter,
it is always some creature or other

and no flesh will enter her mouth,
nor milk, nor egg
and she will brook no cruelty, no swerving

and she may change
since everything changes
but not Her that is passing through her
like a cool wind
full of pine-scent and stone,
a force in iron filings

just so

you are your eye
your eye goes through you

skin, bones, teeth, words,
thoughts, actions, love

every part of you is your eye

Twelfth Night

Twelve days you've been away.
Last night
I couldn't sleep
for thinking about things undone,
wrote notes in the dark
as if you'd never left,
fooling no one.

Sometime around two or three
I heard our neighbour
climbing the stairs next door
and falling heavily into bed,
then muffled voices.
I don't know what they said.

Much later it seemed to me
I heard the stars
clamber to their places,
clouds
rustle loudly as they passed

later still
the Moon
saying something about the Earth,
the wind
asking the trees where you'd gone.

The Way Back

Your sleeping my bridge
over the abyss of night,
each out-breath a plank.

Deer

This morning, waking, almost
absent-mindedly, she
rubbed herself against me,
much as a deer might against a
spruce or maple trunk,
then, dressing by the window,
moved into the winter day
leaving me, metaphorically,
standing, marvelling at the
snow-light on her.

Song for Teja

Four years together,
and almost two of them married,
a large group of people to dinner,
and so much to say and to listen to, you'd think
I could show more constraint with you,
but ever since you came into the room I
can't take my eyes off you.

I don't know if it's your mouth, your lips,
or the glow of your skin,
the shape of your shoulders,
the cut of your hair, or just a word
that is seeming to hang in the air
as if waiting to be said by you, but I
can't take my eyes off you.

If a deer had just walked into the room
or the snow begun to fall
I couldn't take my eyes off you.
If the Southerly had just arrived
on a scorching day, or the first scent of jasmine
had just announced spring
it would still be too hard a thing.

There seems to be no answer
or anything else I can do; even when you're out of sight
I can't take my eyes off you.
Even in bed, much later,
when I've closed them and turned out the light,
through every valley, every cranny of the night,
I can't take my eyes off you.

The Quarry

Reading *Maud* for the first time, so many years late, this
opening passage where the hero
remembers the death of his father in the
blood-edged hollow, I remember that
hot-as-hell summer afternoon
in the quarry outside Queanbeyan, half a lifetime gone,
when a huge boulder I was standing on – told
by the boss to drill two
one-metre holes in it, ready for blasting – began
to shift and I with it, and I
leapt, scrambled, god-
wrenched myself off
and watched it as I slid and tumbled
down seventy feet of rock and shale and it
careered over and over beside me, smashing
the jack-hammer and bending the thick steel bit, so we'd find later,
    a perfect ninety degrees
and I found myself on my feet, at the foot of the slope, not
knowing how, shaking and stunned, the whole
place echoing with a thunderous, ringing silence that seemed to
enter my head then and has never since really gone,
the boulder come to rest less than a foot from the giant
compressor almost exactly its size – and I walked then, turned
the boss's beloved machinery off, and sat, did nothing,
    violently, angrily, stubbornly nothing
until that idiot came,
and answered nothing while he looked, thought, saw
the bit bent at its perfect angle, the huge
gauge down the quarry-side,

and all that he could think to do
was take me for a beer or two
and sit there sullenly staring
thanking God, and wrongly,
that his total exposure had not been exposed.

Something
gave me to you then, though I had no way of knowing it, and you
to me, me
to myself, and all I had for prescience
was a wild exhilaration, oh
but so wild, so
ruthless and so secretly determined that it's
only now – tongue
loosened at last, a torrent and a raging
tumult of years come
to rest a full
third of a century later in the sudden
astonishing calm of you – that it begins to
name itself or
tell me what it is.

Pater Noster[6]

Our Father
who art in heaven
stay there
and we'll stay down here
in the mess you have left for us,
this bright and hideous confusion, the only
heaven there is or ever was and the only hell,
so intertwined they are almost indivisible,
here amongst the corruption and murder and the nevertheless
invincible glory,
the assassinations and the lying, the grief and the
daily amazement, the poverty and affluence, the anger and
ignorance, the cruelty and unexpected
gentleness, sun in the park and bird-flight
and the cool breeze from the harbour
and the papers and the air-waves full of death and repetition

we'll stay here
where the nations clash in their incomprehensible military psychosis,
letting their own people starve
while the guns and the makers of guns, the ravenous makers
devour and devour,
here where twenty-two humans killed in an ambush is
international news but the slaughter of one hundred
million animals each day to feed their slaughterers goes unmentioned
like the guilty secret it is that the whole
civilisation rides upon
(you a slaughterer, I a slaughterer, she, he, all of us, yet the very
mention is blasphemy)

and the moon too rises, strange and beautiful over everything,
sometimes white-silver, sometimes yellow as butter (and red, that
  astonishing red, and people gathered on the street corners
gazing upward, searching for syllables and giving them up, taking their
silence home like a secret longing, some of them citing you, that
waste of mind, that emptiness – this no prayer after all, but rhetoric,
  a frame, a
conversation with an empty box …)

here where the slugs
gather about the dog's bowl while the dog
sleeps in his nest on the armchair
and the spiders on the balcony and in the
corner of the bedroom
weave their miraculous webs – out in the park catching the rain
  or the night's dew, glistening

where two out of five
are so blind there's no seeing,
so lost in themselves there's no
finding any way out
or anything but themselves
(and I, a poet, no excusing …) and we are all of us, all
numbed by the narcotics of our culture, the news and the
  misinformation, the
art and the music, the opera, the jazz, the movies, the
gossip and vicarious living distracting each one of us from the
horrors and our place in them (and if you think this strange
in a love poem think again, love so
uncontainable the tax on it is anger, outrage, speaking: the
deal of it, the contract …)

here with the flood of work and the tumult and kaleidoscope of days,
the darma and the karma, the maya and the greater illusions,
the shouting right now from the fight in the laneway
and the garlic shoots appearing amongst the parsley

here where I sleep so soundly some nights and others
lie awake long into the early morning
thinking about such things, the in-
explicable and unorderable tides of them
and her sleeping beside me, her calm
in-breath and exhalation
the only rod and staff and
explanation I
know now, or need.

Yes

At almost 2.30 am, when you
came to bed
and started
taking off your clothes
I thought I had found a way at last.

You know how, just before we die,
our whole life is supposed to flash before our eyes?
Well, should that happen, then we'd have,
while it is flashing,
to come to that moment when our whole life
flashes before our eyes,
and, while that is happening
all over again, we'd come again
to that same moment,
which is only to say that, while I know
that might have been good enough for Zeno
and that it's certain that death happens anyway, for that one
minute, when that thought
came
and I imagined
living this life over and over,
I said to myself, despite
all the effort, all the pain,
despite
all that has happened
and is likely to
again and again,
Yes, I thought, as I was watching you,

Yes, though I knew it
even then
to be crazy beyond measure,
Yes, I think I will, Yes,
I know I will, Yes.

FROM *Urban Elegies* 2007

HEAD LICE

Each morning
for six days now, warm from her bed,
my ten-year-old daughter
has come to sit by the window
and talk quietly, watching the sparrows
while the kettle boils,
shifting her head without bidding
while I run my fingers
through her fine, soft hair, searching it
strand by strand
to find nothing
but the occasional abandoned egg case
clinging to the root,
or freckle
on the snow-white scalp
amongst my own sudden memories
of childhood on the Cotter River
or birch trees in a Cleveland winter,
or, waiting in ambush, the fought-
back, un-
thinkable certainty
that such moments must end
all too soon now
and will never come again.

Golden Tongues

Poems
come and go like a once-
or twice-a-year season

four or five
in a rush
and then nothing

you think
they're easy
and get careless

but then
you turn around
and the words aren't there

as if you've had your chance at Pentecost
and blown it
and the golden tongues are gone

then
out of the blue
it happens again

life
rising out of nowhere,
needing you for something – an errand – urgently.

Sublime Point

Standing at
Sublime Point, looking out,
is like death
or sudden viciousness, access
to a beauty
you'd never thought you'd have,
an idea that changes everything.

Rock-shelves
crumble into the distant scrub,
birds
dive into a sea of hieroglyphs
dense as an empty page.

Standing at
Sublime Point
you find yourself
longing for the arrival of the lost,
a cure for the illness you think you will die from,
someone to hold you
who will excite you forever

clinging
too fast to the guardrail
as if it were a strong
line around you, a second skin
holding the vastness in.

Menindee

Today it is
dark clouds
moving steadily in from the west,
a deep brown-purple, the colour of the sky
before a sand-storm on the desert's edge.
A dog is barking somewhere
as if to frighten it away.
I realise that I should go around the house
shutting the doors and windows
and bring in the washing from the line,
but now there is a sudden, eerie coldness
like the dip
before a great wave
catches and hurls you upwards.

Poem Beginning with Nothing

You look for something
and you cannot find it; you wake up
and that person is no longer there
and there is no getting them back.

I gather from this that losing
is one of the patterns of being
just as birth is, and dying,
and that we must learn to embrace it

as we welcome food, say, or spring;
that one of the secrets of living, here, now,
is probably the mastery of such, a kind
of art of the *maya*

writing poems
in a language that cannot do,
or loving someone you can't ever know
with a heart you can never rely on

walking to the window
on days such as this
and drawing
a deep breath

turning around,
placing one
foot
carefully in front of the other.

Bird Song

There's a species of
grey and white pigeon
in Glebe, New South Wales,
that lies on its back in the roadway
while traffic passes over it.

The soft feathers
of its breast and
wingtips
riffle in the slipstream
of buses and the
four-wheel drives some like to call
'Balmain Bulldozers'.

The traffic is loud
and hard to listen through.
The delicate beaks
and fragile
skull-bones, the
tiny, intricate feet
under the
dark
rubber tyres
make sounds that
nobody can ever hear.

Barnyard Revelation Poem

An academic poetician friend
while discussing my
barbarous adventures
tells me that he hopes I won't fall victim
to the endemic *poematosis* of the region, by which, as he explains,
he means the writing
of 'barnyard revelation poems'.
I haven't laughed so much in years.
I suppose, instead, I should be producing
postmodern supermarket odes, or linguo-spatiological
poematographs of the
secret life of words – the kinds of things
a close analysis of 'intimate' might intimate, or the way
'impact' can become 'impacted', as if
the postmodern supermarket were anything much other
than sawn-up, mashed, sliced, bottled or deep-
frozen barnyard
or the forms and paraforms, traces and
fathomless abysses of words were any more
than the cum- and pain- and joy-cries
of farmers and their
wives and children, buried under
layer upon layer of the tangled Western Mind.

A Curse

The incomprehensible bastards next door
have sprayed poison
from one end of our garden to the other.
Apparently half a gallon of some
as-yet-to-be-identified pesticide
has been found preferable to a phone call or a five-minute visit
to ask if we might trim a vine.

The seven magenta impatiens are dead,
and the two five-year-old goldfish.
The waterlily that bloomed for the first time this year,
and all the other fish-pond plants
have blackened and sunk beneath the filmy surface.
Green leaves from the Boston Creeper drop down second by second
in a sudden, unnatural autumn. Now, I suppose,
we should fear even the rain
for the way it will spread the poison through the rest.

The dwarf conifer, the box-bush,
the laurel, the basil and parsley,
the thyme and tarragon and oregano,
the chilli plants, the galangal, the lemongrass, the six
proud native irises are all
withering before our eyes
and we can only guess as yet
about the earthworms, caterpillars, skinks,
crickets, praying mantises, slugs, slaters, snails,
or the fate of any birds that might have eaten
from this treacherous buffet.

Beyond confirming yet again the ubiquity
and mundanity of evil
what have they achieved?

Let this then be a curse upon them:
Let them continue to be
self-exiled from the earthly heaven.
Let them never find
such a garden within themselves.
Let there at least be poetic justice.
Let them never understand such
fury, such sadness as this.

The Old Children's Hospital

Thursday morning 6 am, a carefully
unheralded explosion
brings down the tall, red-brick incinerator-tower
of the old Children's Hospital but can do
nothing for the contaminated ground – all the lost,
burned parts of children, limbs, appendixes, cancerous growths
removed from livers, stomachs, brain, the
dressings and the papers and
the blood-soaked sheets all
purged by fire, the radiation and the sickness and despair
entering the soil so deeply that,
January, 2005, developers
still can't offer their sky-
scraping water-views or even
sell the seventeen state-of-the-art
townhouses already built on Alma Street – Johnson's Creek
for ninety years now
trickling under the lot: Kirkaldy House, the playground, the
incinerator block – issuing at the bottom of Wigram Road
in a holy, holy slime.

What is the hold-up?
Could someone be
worried at the
tremulous souls of the lost
haunting the lifts and stairwells? clinging like moths
to the windowsills and
light-sensitised, omni-directional Scandanavian blinds
of the two-income professional couples, invading like pernicious damp

the underground-garaged
RAV4s and SUVs of the young and
upwardly mobile?

Have they heard, perhaps,
the screams and the
sobbing, the pleas
and the terrified whispers
under the stones, riddling the
bark of the trees?

How Not to Be a Cosmologist

Backing into the lane at midday
on the way to the Fisher Library, turning off
the suddenly-too-loud radio
the last thing I hear
is that we are about to talk to a famous
cosmologist.

A cosmologist?
How can that be?
I know that an *astronomer*
is technically a namer of stars
and that an *astrologist* tries to make sense of them
the way a soap opera
makes sense of history
or the mess one has made of one's marriage
but the notion of an expert
in the logic of the Cosmos
seems suddenly strange to me
as if someone could really be
a specialist in Everything
or, if they could, would be much different
from a poet, say,
or the tumbling universe inside one of the trucks
of the Leichhardt Municipal Council's
Waste Collection service.

An *astronomer* friend of mine
tells me that she studies parts
but a *cosmologist* studies the whole.

I don't mean to doubt her
but how can there be
a whole that isn't inside another one?
and how can a study of wholes
be anything other than a study of parts?
if a whole is everything, then how can
everything be all there is?

It seems, at the very least, that studying the Cosmos
would have some serious problems of scale, like trying
to reconstruct the Second World War
from a matchbox found in Alaska
or the entire Serengeti Game Park
from inside a parasite
inside a wart in an elephant's ear.

In my short life I must have heard
twenty-five different theories of the cosmos
and although you might think
twenty-five different cosmologists
couldn't be wrong
twenty-four of them were sure
the other twenty-four were
which isn't completely to dismiss the possibility
that one of them might
one day come up with something
although I myself would make no claims, nor think
sitting out in the courtyard
late on New Year's Eve 2001
looking up at the sky
and imagining that the vast sheet of cloud
slipping by under the

almost-full moon
was like a ghostly Soviet army
marching past Joseph Stalin
on May Day 1937
would rate very highly
as an example of the discipline.

The theory I like
is the one that says that everything that is
is just ancient light arriving
after millions of years –
even me, even the cosmologist, even this poem –
and that the world
is no more than another screen
erected by Atlas Copco
in an endless cinema
called, let's say, *The Majestic*
or *The Infinite Starlight Drive-in.*

Rat Theses

There's a rat in the compost
she tells me, as she comes in from the yard;
it jumped out when she lifted the lid
and used her forearm as a springboard
into a pile of leaves.
I know it's my job to kill it
after all I've got a reputation,
thirty-three rats in less than a fortnight,
and although that was seventeen years ago
and in another city, maybe it's also
my civic duty; there was bubonic plague
on Sussex Street once, and for all I know
rats carry a dozen other diseases:
cholera, dysentery, typhoid fever, not to mention
enteritises
or strange malfunctions of the mind.

I go out and buy a trap
but it's raining when I get home
and I put it in the cupboard
while I think about where to set it.
Weeks go by. My wife and the rat
come to a kind of understanding:
she makes some noise
as she approaches the compost
and it doesn't use her as a springboard.
Eventually it doesn't even come out of its hole
and I imagine it lying there, under the warm
lawn clippings, waiting for its daily

shower of scraps
that must be like a rain
of giant caesar salad bits, or shards
of a seventeen-foot papadum
delivered by the North Indian Diner.

Sometimes,
when I wake at night,
I think of the rat
coming out of its hole
and sniffing the air, checking the moonlight
for signs of an owl or tawny frogmouth,
wondering whether it's safe
to go for a walk, listening intently
for the stealthy nosings of a feral cat.

I don't
think I want to kill it; it
seems too much like myself.
What, after all, does a rat
symbolise?
and if I kill it
what have I made of me?

No,
I don't want to kill it. It is only
eating our vegetable scraps, and it doesn't
seem to be breeding.
I think I would get it
a bubonic inoculation if I could
and as for the other diseases,
they can't be too much worse

than someone sneezing on a crowded bus
or a couple of human strangers
naked in bed.

And ratness?
I don't know.
Sometimes, when I look
at my face in the mirror,
I catch a kind of ratness in the eyes,
just as once, when I stared into the eyes
of some of the thirty-three dead
there was, very clearly, a *me*.

I'm sure there are times when
the rat's suspected
cats in the ranks, or regretted
its own owl-like behaviour – times, like me,
when it's sniffed the wind
and decided not to answer the door,
times when it's thought
there are huge
humans there
I don't want to go out.

Flute Music

Cool flute music
enters the courtyard
and enters every thing
living or dead

it enters the children
and comes out as laughter

it enters the peacocks
and comes out a thousand eyes

it enters the pigeons
that all day
have fussed about the statue of St Francis

unable to stop it
or turn it into song
they rise
above the high red roofs
and bank towards the sea

Night Rain

Rain, hard rain, long after midnight.
We wake, and sleep, and wake again,
sometimes in sorrow, sometimes pain,
sometimes from dreams to find more dreams gone,
the body and the life readjusting, limbs
twining and turning apart
in the ebbing and the flowing of the heart.

It continues, in great walls and brushes,
sweeping forgotten places, chartless
hinterlands of memory or blame, thinning slowly
to the after-rain from branches, lingering
until the first birds come, until at last,
on clean streets, gleaming pavements,
day breaks open, everything begins again.

Pentecost

At Moody's, the Wharf Hotel,
in the last small village on the Head,
a man is reading poetry aloud.
Until last night, until he said
that he was leaving,
we'd known him only as the one
who stood sometimes at dusk
on Ocean Beach, casting
for whiting and for silver bream
and then came in to drink a beer or two
in the half an hour before closing –
until, that is, someone had asked
just what it was he did all day
shut away in his tiny weatherboard
or simply sitting in the yard.

Now, responding
to our half-request,
he is sitting on a high stool at the far end of the bar
and all the rest of us are standing round,
sceptical at first, but slowly strangely moved
to find our Head a place of mystery and dark.
Who would have guessed
that such serenity could rise
from boats and nets we used all day
or that we could feel such sudden, unfamiliar love
for things we'd never seen?
Who would have dreamt
such beauty, or such bristling life

lay hidden in the promontory scrub,
or thought that on that beach
a man could talk so readily to God?

Between the poet's hands, it seems, appear
not papers, but rustling birds, or fish
that move as if the smoky light
were water, or were shifting leaves.
The pages turn, and on them are not sounds
but things, not lines
but memories and dreams:
worlds open, where we'd thought were fields
and teeming forests where we thought were trees;
forgotten loves, like great red flowers
bloom painfully within us
and slowly our sceptics, like our joking, cease.

Later, when Moody
has reluctantly called time,
we issue down the wooden steps
and quickly scatter in the dark
impatient to hold our sleeping children
or to see again
our oldest, most familiar things
convinced that they have somehow changed.
Tomorrow, perhaps, not all may think so,
but tonight,
in a dozen darkened rooms across the Head,
the unaccustomed words will circle us
like feathers, or like flashing fins
or a hundred other visitings
of sudden, unexpected light.

FROM *Walking to Point Clear* 2005

DINNER AT MIDNIGHT

Dinner at midnight,
the baby
finally asleep;
we talk softly for an hour
and listen
in the spaces between
to all the small sounds of the house
become now so suddenly larger:
the refrigerator humming,
the candle
guttering in its well of wax,
and something else
gathering about us,
a white silence
like snow on deep water,
this house
an ocean vessel of sorts,
rigging
of joists and weatherboard,
sails
of bedsheets, eiderdown.

The Pines, Cottesloe

Firetails
tunnel through banksia,
worms
bore into bast and phloem
or turn about the dark root
half-blind in earthblack.

Behind the house
in a stand
of tall radiata
white cockatoos
are ripping the tight young
pine cones into flight.

Beneath them
between trunks
already knee-deep in twilight
a garden spider
is weaving a huge night star
and I can hear
in the long grass
something stirring.

Already
in twos and threes
the gulls are returning
and one late crow
labouring like a man in mid-channel.

For a moment
retracing the path
I am half in love
even with his dark wings, coal-
black and shining,
coming back
again and again
at nightfall
to rest in the high pines.

Eschatology

for Richard Exner

Mind
dwells on apocalypse,
the body digs

the shutting of a gate,
the turning of a sod, a page
once done is
done, a work complete

the change,
the travelling
come down to this,
the great circle of days,
recurrence of the simplest things.

Between two slabs
I dig a wine-cellar,
floor it with brick,
wall it
with brick and board

soon I will stock it, build
a new shed over it,
soon
the eggplants will rise, tomatoes
push up behind the basil,
and my child will be walking.

You write from California
astonished at my faith in Things.

What can I say?

There is a place, a border
where chill leaves the words,
where even the fire leaves
and all that is said becomes hopeless.

Deeper still
there is a place where it begins again.

Valparaíso

I laid you down
and moved your dress aside
and tasted
between your thighs
the sweet vinegars of Valparaíso.

How many hours ago
did the wind start
buffeting the skylight
filling the deckchairs
with snow?

Lemons

Lemons
are the world's fruit,
the most democratic and versatile,
an edible gold, a liquid spice.

They whiten hands,
they remove stains from clothing,
they flavour a thousand dishes.

In the right climate,
with little encouragement,
they crop
seven times in a year.

Fresh picked
they will sit in a bowl for ages
filling the air with their fragrance.

The smell
of a lemon
at midday
is like a cool breeze from the sea.

At dusk
from the grove
at the bottom of the farm
the lemons glow
like ghostly green lanterns.

Crows sing of lemons,
children
run about the hot yard
clutching lemons in their hands.

Old women
in black dresses
sit
with golden lemons in their laps,
their eyes closed,
their minds
far away with the scent of lemons.

Mosquitoes

After sunset
the heat takes up residence indoors

we move outside
and watch the lightning
craze the Pacific
hear late birds
cry in the pitch dark

asleep or awake
we listen all night to the ocean
dream it is
the roll and crash of stars

mosquitoes
graze on our nakedness
leave at dawn
through the frayed screens
taking their tiny cargoes of our blood
into the great fields of light

their sound
by midday
the drone of chainsaws, cars on the highway

Depot Elegy

The retired sawmiller, great arsehole,
has ploughed a road through the cycads
and that is the beginning of an end to it.
His three-storey brick-and-tile monstrosity
cranes out of the hillside
and the whine of his chainsaw or grind
of his four-wheel drive as he hauls
his fourteen-footer from the boat ramp
can be heard any day of the year.
Now a sign has appeared outside Moores Cabins,
a small thing, but you can see it
all the way from Point Clear
and my heart sinks at its confirmations.

All afternoon
on the south rocks
we were casting into the rising water
catching nothing
and yet in my childhood I remember
bream, trevally, parrotfish, yellowtail, gar
and a dozen others I could list
and once
from the wharf at Huskisson
a mullet run that had my mother weeping.
Now the coast, they say,
is more or less fished out
all the way down to Bermagui
and I am barely forty.

All night I have lain here
listening to the owls
and the plash of wallabies in the undergrowth
watching the stars through the window-screens,
feeling a different cold
rising from the pole,
the whole Earth
rolling towards a new extinction
devoured by such sudden parasites
(and I am one),
another, deeper night beginning
even here
and going out over the forest
and the forest with it:
the echidna in his bolt-hole,
the eagle
on the headland
high over the midden and the vanished fires,
the lyrebirds on Mount Agony,
the great monitor,
wallabies, kangaroos, quolls,
all of us
wrapped in this lasting, this
absolute night,
and every one of them expecting morning.

FROM BACK AFTER EIGHT MONTHS AWAY

THE FIRE

Full moon
and the tin roofs of the holiday houses
lit up like silver.
Watched by a possum from the top of Lahey's tank
who will later come down
for potato skins, charred
slivers of onion or capsicum,
I build a small fire on the mound of stones
and stand there almost mesmerised,
feeding it chunks
of ironbark, boxwood, spotted gum
and after them words,
watching it tear them into flame.

BUSH MOUSE

Night-stirrer,
raider of cupboards and open drawers,
skater across polished floorboards, relentless
worrier of barricades, gnawing itself bloody
for the skerricks of humans, the bush mouse
likes Easter eggs, pistachio nuts, tubes
of Deadant, the cardboard and plastic
of tack-packets, parcels of screws,
but most of all – true
bastard of Irish
convict stock – potatoes, new
potatoes, small

and round
and hard enough
to hold in its determined paws
and crunch as, intently, passionately, ears
cocked wide for a movement from the bedroom,
it stares out the window at the giant moon.

Lyrebird

Early
on the way to a meeting in Bateman's
I glimpse a lyrebird
on the edge of the Mt Agony road
gone as soon as I notice it

I slow down
and look at the place where it entered
but there is nothing,
the bird
become dry branch, scrub-
shadow.

Later
writing this down
I wonder what part of the self it is
hides amongst language

looking at
these words, this
page,
trying to find where I entered.

The Forest Within Us

One time we went down
and it was the coldest it had ever been,
the sea wild and
no fishing to be had,
the skies bright blue most days
but a breeze
straight from the pole,
moonless nights burning with stars.

On the deck one afternoon
I looked up from my reading
and there were a hundred birds:
king parrots, bowers, mountain lowries, currawongs
and one I hadn't seen for years
coming back again and again
for whatever we could find for it,
the forest alive with wrens.

Poetry? No.
It had gotten past that;
but there were irrepressible words:

at night I would lie awake
and listen to the surf
and the forest rustlings,
waiting for the first
slip of light through the curtains,
not writing
thinking almost of nothing.

So Little

Five years before the end of the century
and the poetry still no easier,
subjects
still faltering, images
still fleeing the grasp,
the weight of the body shifting,
emphases all falling differently.

Who would have thought
so much could come to so little?
A subtler sense
of the indefinite article, infinitives
that will not be split
by anything: patience, work, suffering,
not even love.

A Cry

Why should the cosmos, hearing
one thing
complaining against another,
take notice,
since every thing,
even death,
is a part of itself?

Isn't it the one thing
that nothing leaves?
If I cry out
just once
doesn't that cry go on forever?

Without Warning

My father spent most of his working life
in the Commonwealth Public Service, shunting files
from one end of his long desk to the other.
When he died he left half-written
a *History of Australian Immigration*,
only half-joking when he willed that I should finish it.
Why didn't he tell me
how little would ever be completed?
letters left unanswered, accounts not settled, promises
never fulfilled, the parts of that motorcycle
un-reassembled, lying ten years
on a concrete floor in Westgarth Street, people
dying without warning, mid-sentence,
taking the next words with them.

Fire and Ice

Midwinter
on the other side of the world.
Sometime during the night
an inaudible clock
struck the hour I can never remember
and I turned a year older.
I woke, just the once,
to some strange movement in the house
and didn't think of it
nor of my mother
heaving herself to the bus to Manuka
to bring the labour on
succumbing to caesarean the next day
while the bushfires ringed Black Mountain,
losing ovaries, uterus,
and so much else
that she and I were never right, not really,
the flame that crept in when they opened her
in the gaping light as I was lifted out
smouldering ever afterward,
twisting us
this way and that
so we could never touch without burning.

Here
it is cold out,
deer
walk over the frozen lawn;
in the late night

you can hear their gentle rubbings
against tree trunks, fence posts.
On a fire trail
in the wood beyond the highway
I point out their footprints
to my nine-year-old daughter
and the flame-red crest of the woodpecker
its sudden loud feverish knocking
high on the side of a barn.

Later,
coming in to the warm,
stamping the crusted snow from our boot-soles,
her brown eyes wide and
gleaming with cold,
she asks me to feel her frozen hands
then holds my fingers to her face
to feel her cheeks,
how hot they are, how burning.

The Vision of Saint Eustace

Four weeks ago a wind
straight from Siberia
scraped through the square
snapping the leaves off plane trees,
hiding the village
behind closed shutters, curtained doors.
Now, the weather milder, nearing Christmas,
small boys are kicking footballs
in the Place Jeu de Ballon
while their fathers
trim vines beyond Tressan
or play petanque behind the Mairie
and Madam Sabatier's brother Robert
sits on his bench
with his one yellow glove
shooting imaginary pigeons from the air.
Straight
from *The Vision of Saint Eustace*
a young brown dog, too
callow for the hunt
runs down the Impasse des Cigales
with a stolen croissant.
A few *granates*
still cling to the winter bushes; the path
to Le Puget
is strewn with fallen almonds.
In the field by the highway
the pheasants
have nested over the ancient icehouse.

After the thunder
of the Mirage *chasseur*
a slender glider
drifts soundless through the light-grey sky.
In the White House, half
a century away,
the President wipes his prick,
declares another war against Iraq;
on the tarmac, 'intelligent' missiles sit
in cold and steely silence, unable to think
of what they are about to do.

FROM *The Cold Front* 1983

The Gap

On the pond path by Campbell's
amidst the wheel-ruts and the fallen leaves
a gap nothing fills

it gets late

birds
cross in the half-light
lugging their haul towards Tumut
Bimberi
Kosciuszko
the great lake of silence beneath them

flight after flight after flight

The Promises[7]

We have come
to the short days
and the great circle of shadow,
the hills whitening, the colour
vanishing from the grass.

Already I have seen
the last geese
arc over the waste, the last
ox-cart
wind down from Nan-So.

Nights in this place
I cannot sleep
for thoughts of the lost loves, the great
novels of the south; Pine Island, Sun Street.

But it is not the street girls
that I think of
now, when wind moans in the guys
and the fire scatters
and the bones
of the poplars
thresh their silver in the blackness.

I lift a smooth stone from the ashes
and put it to my ear
and hear nothing,
only somewhere

far below
the dam breaking, roots
taking their soundings,
the ancient
weaving and unweaving of the promises.

Dragon-Fly

The heavens are lasting, earth
endures without end,
but bad news comes from the south:
the sparrows starve, the blue racoon
weeps blood, the eyes
of the owl
grow over.

Lying out by the reservoir
I watch you dive
through the fishflies, islands
of abandoned wings

here too
the body
suddenly trembling.

I rise, of course, and call to you,
the sap
of no colour
rising in the trees

the Great Dragon-Fly of Li Ho
setting out
just before rain.

THE COLD FRONT

It was coming

the cold front
and the complex weather

we returned
and the difficult lives were waiting

the long conversations
with pain in the final sentences

winter
gathering her parcel for the victory

stones, feathers, bottles
brimming with light

the troops
breaking through the syllables

the empty cups
sitting before us in the snow

this
like all the others

a lullaby

a few grains of salt at the centre

A Cut

the thin
trail of down
from your navel

the faint
scar
like a buff of silk at your elbow

why do you go from me
piecemeal?

a cut of the hair, a dress

Montevideo

A small brass band rehearses in a side-street.
A breeze blows in from the Platte.
Crowds
gather in the square before the house.

At last
you appear on the balcony
the dress you wear
barely veiling your miraculous body.

Everyone claps

the band
breaks onto the thoroughfare

over the square
a few pigeons set out for Rio.

Sei Mountains Poem

Four days since you watered the sunflowers.

I am out
in the long grass by the poplars
and there is a light at your window.

Over the dragon-screen
in the room where you sleep
mist gathers in the Mountains of Sei.

I feel
like a small cricket in the grass.

It is a thousand miles to your door.

Compost Quinces

1

In late summer
under the compost quinces
worms
turn in the broken melons
maggots feed
in the cat skull
the hard blue wings
of blowflies
glitter like chain mail

2

Torn
arguments, crushed
sermons, vows
broken in the seventh month

in the neap-
tide of the blood
flies
wash and withdraw

Sometimes
you can hear
the slow dance at the edge
the small, hard bits
and all around
the unconscious *Gaudete* of vanishing

3

Once
in mid afternoon
when the birds had gone
and the possum
slept in the quinces
the one tune
was the reassuring soft buzz-saw of rot

I could feel the shards
of all I had crushed
or hated

muscle
working to free them
or actual song
scouring and scouring the heart

4

Amico, in the midst of poetry
we are vanishing,
I do not claim it is simple

But sometime, after all,
we all take off
the clothes of mistrust

and crawl, or are crawled,
naked into god
sans tie, *sans* shoes, *sans* overcoat

and lie
like still, still fruit

You could say, like it or not,
we all have the same last words
written on our lips

brother worm
brother maggot
brother rot

My Grandfather's Silence

My mother sits in the lounge-room
watching TV

she clenches her handkerchief
and sips tea that has brewed since mid-morning

Her father stalks in the garden
carrying a small red trowel

he is king of the side-paths
and my mother knows it

They grapple in utter silence
for the rest of the house

the right to vacuum
and to scour the cups

Sometimes I cannot sleep
for her moving about in the kitchen

Sometimes when I wake
I feel I am at the centre of my grandfather's silence

I stare at the first light
as it comes through the bedroom window

and I can see the oaks on Westgarth Street
and smell the wisteria
whoever's house it is

whoever's damned garden

The Swineflower

Stars,
sunflowers,
I am eating life,
my life and the lives of others,
births and marriages, separations,
the ecstasies of copulation, death
I grow full but I carry on
I become ill but I persevere

My appetite amazes me
and frightens my friends
Doctors listen to my racing heart
How can a creature eat like this?
How can the belly stand it?

I continue
I tear at it and snort
I slurp ostentatiously
letting it dribble from my chin
I gulp great draughts of darkness
and they do not pain me

One by one my companions
reach satiety and go
I visit them at midnight
and trawl my fat through their garbage
Nothing escapes me

I am the truffler,
the finder of diamonds
I am the pearler-in-shit
Such bitter muscle and bone!
Such sweetness!

Gorged on love, on sadness
I stand in the empty square
and yawp my vast confusions to the moon
I vomit, and weep, and eat again

Later
when all else is denied me
I feed myself to myself
I grow thin and hard
My eye-teeth peer from my jowl
I can feel the seeds
of all I have eaten
sprouting from my bowel

Someday
even if it must be the day of my dying
petals will spring from my orbits
leaves will burst from my breast and thighs
and a bright, adamantine stamen
will issue from my rotting tongue

Someday
on a patch of the heart-stained ground
you will find
in the lightening gloom
the swineflower, the carnivore orchid

and know
that nothing is wasted
that nothing in the long, hot tumult of the swine
is sordid
not even the hunger I died for
not even
for all it has left bare or broken
that strange seed
of sunflower, starflower
flaring in your spine

Holding Up

We were holding

on a cliff, in a clearing

something heavy and difficult

It became important that we keep it in the air,
the higher the better

When one of us left or grew tired, someone else would come

Sometimes, when it rested on our shoulders, we
would watch the leaves turning to flame on the trees,
the sure migration of ants

far before us
the birds crossing over the forest
the mountains
the thin crust of light on the border

And what, after all, were we holding?

The sunset? The wind
heavy with spore from the tableland?

Myrrh?

The Darkness

Once more
uprooted
in the violent arcing of our blood
I roam
my own backcountry
                                    where they lie
like landmines for the revenant

whispered
windy in the tent-flaps, in the
knotted dream
that stirs
the desert birds at midnight
in the long plaint
fluted through the orbits of a steer
far off
          by a creek-bed
                                    scarred
and ghosted by desire

fragments
   that will not alchemise to song
that yield not
   to the metaphrast

that stay
with the boy
in that desert winter
hastening

in the flames by which he sits,
from which he begs
respite and love,
their inescapable loss to blackness

The gene-fire
crackles and subsides,
a chill along the spine
would have me
haunt your sleep again

Late
and in this sudden fear
I touch
the incandescent scarf
that in the leaked light
flickers
over mandible, zygoma

the endurance
of these embers
all I know of morning

O beloved
in the deep night burning
vital and unscarred, my
unaware interpreter
what is it that the wind
whispers to the flames
that they devour the more wildly
seeking their own end?

what is it drives us
over dark savannahs
bewintered and unscored, mouthing
the few short phrases

madsongs

to our ashes?

Notes

1 Although this title refers to a vendor of a very different kind, it recalls Moises Simons's famous rhumba 'The Peanut Vendor' ('El Manisero'), first recorded in 1927 and covered many many times since. Stan Kenton's 1947 version is well known.

2 'Tablelands' was written as part of the 'Shadow Catchers' project highlighting works from the photography collection of the Art Gallery of New South Wales.

3 'Leaping Towards Boston' was written in support of a campaign to persuade major international manufacturers of sports apparel to cease using kangaroo leather in their manufacture of shoes. I recognise that 'k-leather' has been used mainly in the production of soccer cleats, but it seemed at the time of writing that the Boston Marathon might be a better vehicle for the satire. While I am pleased to note that several major manufacturers have decided to cease using kangaroo leather, I note also that, while they did so, 800,000 kangaroos were shot annually to supply them, and that well over three million kangaroos are still shot each year to supply other markets.

4 'Then Allah sent a crow digging up the earth so that he might show him how he should cover the dead body of his brother.' (the Koran).

5 'The Magician' is dedicated to Richard Deutch, poet, magician and friend, who died in 2005. We had sometimes spoken of writing poems based on various magic tricks. The poems in this sequence came to me in the months after his death. Not all of them refer to him.

6 'Pater Noster' takes its title and first three lines from the opening of Jacques Prévert's poem of the same name.

7 The first lines of this poem are loosely translated from the second of Dante's *Rime per la donna pietra* (*Rhymes for the Stone Woman*): 'Al poco giorno e al gran cerchio d'ombra' (poem 101 of his *Rime*).

Acknowledgements

Many of the poems in *The Other Side of Daylight* have appeared in earlier collections of mine: *The Cold Front* (Hale & Iremonger, 1983); *Walking to Point Clear* (Brandl & Schlesinger, 2005); *Urban Elegies* (Island Press, 2007); *The Balcony* (UQP, 2008); and *Open House* (UQP, 2015). I would like to thank and acknowledge these publishers and the many periodicals and anthologies in which the poems from these collections first appeared.

Poems in *The Peanut Vendor* have previously appeared in *Aletheia*, *Australian Poetry Journal*, *Cultural Politics* (Duke University Press), *The Kenyon Review*, *Live Encounters*, *Mascara Literary Review*, *Meanjin*, *Southerly*, and the anthologies *In Case of Fire: Poems from the Blue Mountains* (Spinebill Press, 2022), *The Best Australian Poems 2016* (Black Inc., 2016), *The Best Australian Poems 2017* (Black Inc., 2017), *Best of Australian Poems 2021* (Australian Poetry, 2021), and *Best of Australian Poems 2022* (Australian Poetry, 2022).

So many people have helped, encouraged and supported me in the decades I have been writing that any attempt to name them individually could only end in failure and embarrassment. I thank them all. Thanks are due too to the universities in which I have studied and taught, for their intellectual, artistic and practical support. Thanks are due in particular to The University of Sydney, which continues to support my work with an honorary appointment, and to the Australia Council (now Creative Australia), for a 2015/16 fellowship, the fruits of which are still arriving.